PEOPLE OF THE HEBRIDES
at Home and Abroad
1800-1850

By
David Dobson

CLEARFIELD

Published for Clearfield Company by
Genealogical Publishing Company
Baltimore, Maryland
2020

ISBN 9780806359144

INTRODUCTION

The Hebrides are a small group of islands off the west coast of Scotland. The first half of the nineteenth century in the Hebrides marked a period of major change of society and the economy. During the eighteenth century the Highlands of Scotland experienced a collapse of the traditional structures of society and the economy that was somewhat alleviated by government action. The improvement in the infrastructure, notably the road system, while designed for military purposes, actually, facilitated the cattle trade. Also, harbour improvements intended to develop the fishing industry created jobs and expanded the economy.

The British Government encouraged settlement of British North America, especially by Loyalists and former soldiers after 1783, and by former soldiers and the unemployed after 1815. The second half of the eighteenth century saw a significant increase in the population of the Highlands, one greater than the ability of the local economy to sustain. This pressure contributed to an outflow of population from the Highlands---of which the Hebrides were a part--to the burgeoning industrial towns of Lowland Scotland and England, as well as to the colonies. A major source of employment for these Highlanders was in military service with the British Army during the Seven Years War [the French and Indian War] 1756 to 1763, the American War of Independence, 1776-1783, and the French Wars from 1789 to 1815.

During these campaigns, the Highland economy was stimulated by the demand for cattle, fish, and kelp, but in the aftermath, demand contracted causing unemployment. At the same time the Industrial Revolution was creating a demand for wool for the textile industry. Landowners were encouraged to improve efficiency, which in the Highlands meant the restructure of agricultural lands into more profitable units, especially the merging of small farms or crofts and the expansion of sheep farms. This restructuring of agriculture caused a labour surplus with no alternative work available. By abandoning traditional farming—either by raising rent or by 'clearing the land'-- landowners could generate more income but at a social cost. At the same time the population was increasing, and emigration was an option. The potato blight and the famine of 1837 and 1838 meant that many families were living in poverty. Unemployment, destitution, and the large-scale evictions of the nineteenth century that some landowners practiced in order to clear land for sheep farming were the main reasons for emigration from the Highlands and notably the Hebrides.

This book attempts to identify residents of the Hebrides, especially of the islands of Skye, Islay, Mull, Lewis, and Harris, and Hebrideans who chose to emigrate to the Carolinas, Maritime Canada, and Australia, during the early nineteenth century. Most modern Hebridean placenames are Anglicised versions of the original Gaelic placenames. The Hebrideans were Gaelic speakers so the Gaelic placenames which they would have used have been added. Many of the Gaelic placenames include a Norse element revealing early Scandinavian settlement on the Hebrides. What is different about Highland emigration is that they emigrated as family groups, settling together where they could maintain their Gaelic language, culture, and religion, often in frontier locations such as Cape Breton or the Cape Fear Valley.

David Dobson
Dundee, Scotland, 2020

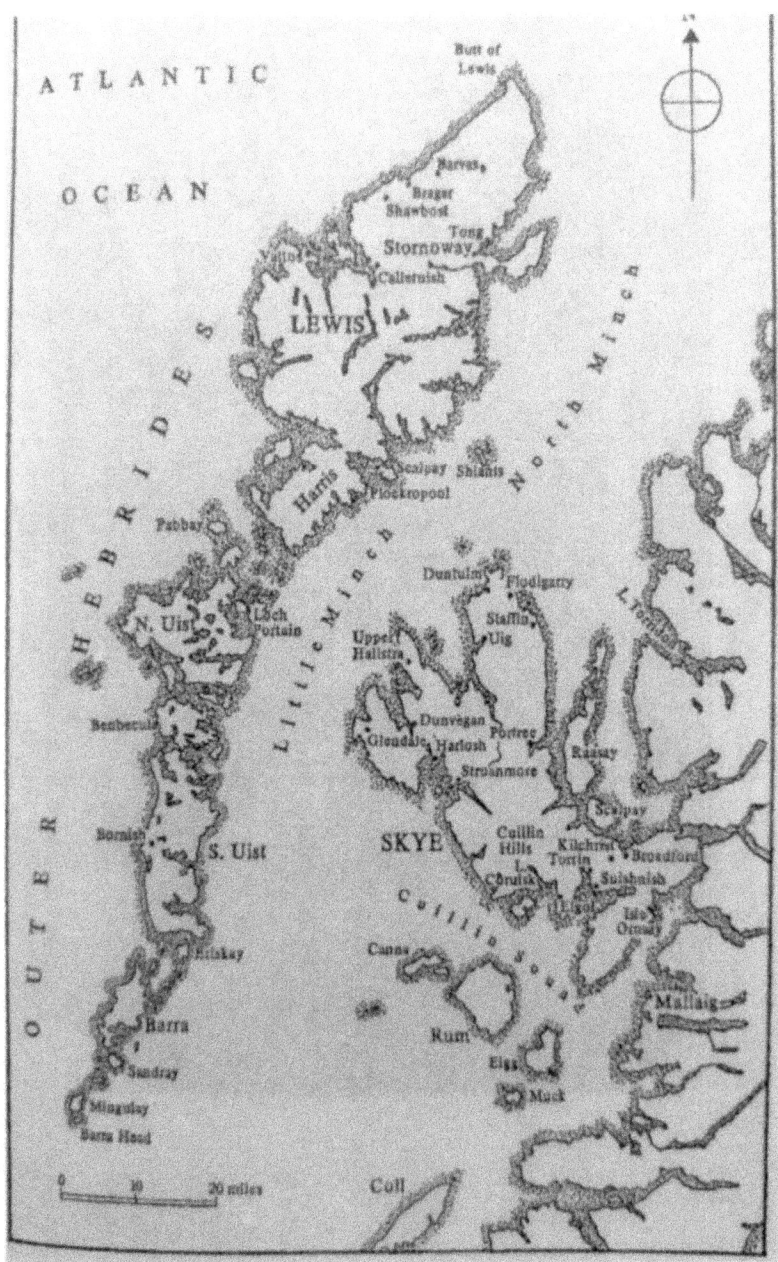

ATLANTIC

OCEAN

Butt of
Lewis

Barvas

Bragar
Shawbost

Tong
Stornoway

Valtos
Callernish

LEWIS

North Minch

Scalpay Shiant
Plockropool

Harris

Pabbay

Little Minch

Duntulm
Flodigarry

N. Uist
Loch
Portain

Staffin
Uig

Upper
Hallstra

Dunvegan
Glendale
Harlosh

Portree

Raasay

Benbecula

Struanmore

Scalpay

Bornish

S. Uist

SKYE

Cuillin
Hills
L.
Scavaig

Kilchrist
Torrin
Suishnish

Broadford

Lochalsh

Isle
Ornsay

Cuillin Sound

Canna

Mallaig

Barra

Rum

Eigg

Sandray

Muck

Mingulay
Barra Head

0   10   20 miles

Coll

OUTER   HEBRIDES

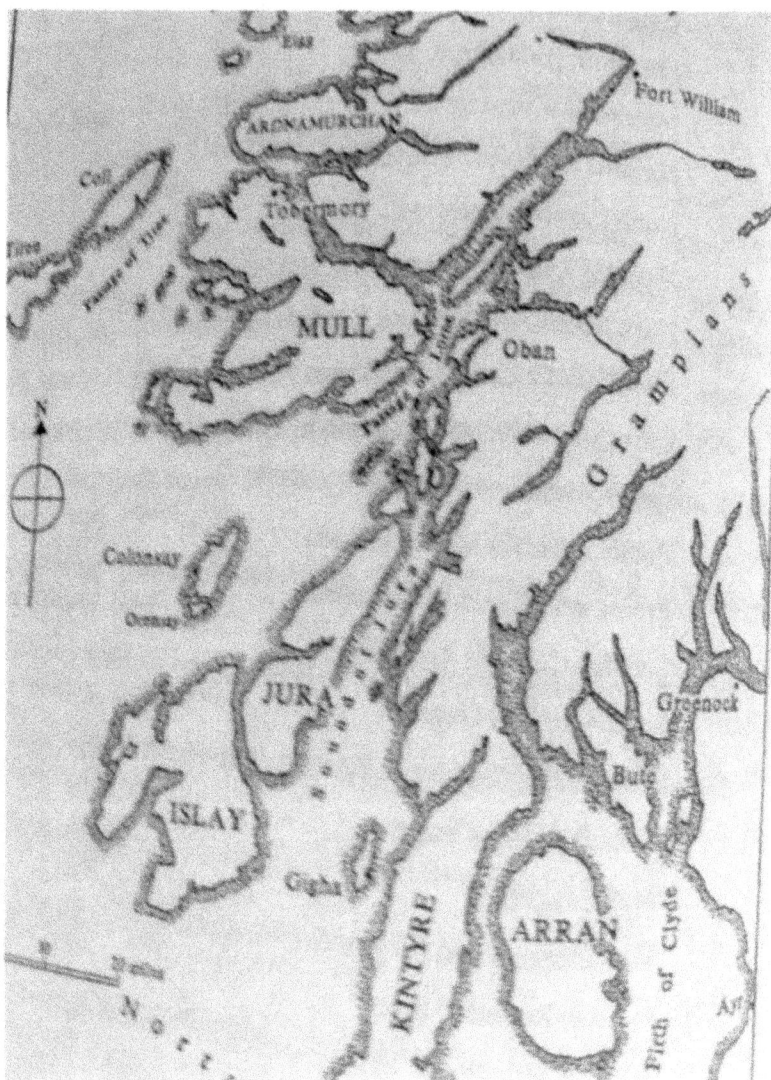

ALLEN, THOMAS, born 1781, Frances Allen born 1781, Thomas born 1802, and Maria born 1804, from Tobermory, Mull, [Tobar Mhoire, Muile] aboard the brig Humpheys bound for Prince Edward Island in 1806. [PAPEI.2702]

ANDERSON, MALCOLM, born on Sleat [Sleite] in 1788, emigrated to North Carolina in 1799, settled in Savanna, Georgia, in 1811, died there on 11 October 1814. [Savanna Republican, 27.10.1814]

BEATON, ALEXANDER, with his wife Mary and children Anne, Kat, Donald, Isabel, and John, from Skye [Sgiathnach] aboard the Malay bound for Sydney, Nova Scotia, in 1830. [NSARM.RG1.67/19]

BEATON, ALEXANDER, born 1824, Margaret born 1825, from Marishadder, Skye, [Sgiathanach] emigrated via Liverpool aboard the Ticonderoga bound for Port Philip, Australia, on 4 August1852. [NRS.HD4/5]

BEATON, ANGUS, born 1797, Mary born 1808, Sally born1830, Donald born 1835, Christy born 1840, Mary born 1842, Neil born 1844, and Mizee born 1846, from Dervaig [Dearbhaig] on the Quinish estate, Mull, [Muile] emigrated via Liverpool aboard the Marmion bound for Moreton Bay, Australia, on 28 August 1852. [NRS.HD4/5]

BEATON, DONALD, with Janet and son Malcolm, from Skye [Sgiathanach] aboard the Malay bound for Sydney, Nova Scotia, in 1830. [NSARM.RG1.67/19]

BEATON, JOHN, with wife Margaret and daughter Mary, from Skye [Sgiathanach] aboard the Malay bound for Sydney, Nova Scotia, in 1830. [NSARM.RG1.67/19]

BEATON, JOHN, with children Anne, John, Betsy, Isabel, and Donald, from Skye [Sgiananach] aboard the Malay bound for Sydney, Nova Scotia, in 1830. [NSARM.RG1.67/19]

BEATON, JOHN, with wife and children, a cottar in Portree, [Port Righ], Skye, applied to emigrate to Australia in 1854. [NRS.GD221.4437/1]

BEATON, MALCOLM, with Mary, from Skye aboard the Malay bound for Sydney, Nova Scotia, in 1830. [NSARM.RG1.67/19]

BEATON, NIALL, with Catherine MacIntyre his wife, Alastair, Domhnull, Seumas, Iain, Catherine, Mairead, etc, from Boisdale, Barra, possibly emigrated on board the Harmony to Cape Breton in 1821.

BEATON, NIEL, from South Uist, emigrated aboard the Emperor Alexander of Aberdeen, master Alexander Watt, from Tobermory, Mull, to Sydney, Cape Breton, in July 1823., landed on 16 September 1823. [Inverness Journal, 30 January 1824]

BEATON, NEIL, born 1798, in Penmore, died 8 November 1843, his wife Sarah McColl, born 1798, died 15 March 1878. [Calgary Bay gravestone, Mull]

BEATON, PETER, born 1819, Anne born 1832, Anne born 1849, from Feull, emigrated via Liverpool aboard the Araminta bound for Geelong, Australia, on 20 May 1852. [NRS.HD4/5]

BEATON, SAMUEL, with his wife Ket, and children Mary and Donald, from Skye aboard the Malay bound for Sydney, Nova Scotia, in 1830. [NSARM.RG1.67/19]

BEATON, WILLIAM, with Mary, and children Donald, Neil, and Janet, from Skye aboard the Malay bound for Sydney, Nova Scotia, in 1830. [NSARM.RG1.67/19]

BEITH, JOHN, factor of Gigha, [Giogha], 1832. [NRS.CS46.1832.1.47]

BELL, ARCHIBALD, born on Colonsay [Colbhasa] in 1774, died on Prince Edward Island on 12 August 1835. [Woods Islands Pioneer Cemetery, P.E.I.]

PEOPLE OF THE HEBRIDES, 1800-1850

BETHUNE, JOHN, with three brothers, one sister, a brother-in-law and his wife, from Fisherfield, Skye, emigrated to Australia on board the Arabian in 1854. [NRS.GD221.4437.1]

BETHUNE, MARION, born 1800, Anne born 1825, Murdoch born 1828, Christy born 1833, Roderick born 1841, Anne born 1838, from Uig, Skye, emigrated via Liverpool aboard the Priscilla bound for Victoria, Australia, on 15 October 1852. [NRS.HD4/5]

BETHUNE, MARY, born in 1828, from Glen Halten, Skye, emigrated via Glasgow on board the Georgiana bound to Port Philip, Australia, on 13 July 1852. [NRS.HD4/5]

BETHUNE, NORMAN, born 1820, Catherine born 1824, Finlay born 1830, Janet born 1848, and Ann born 1850, from Romisdale, [Romasdal], Skye, emigrated via Liverpool aboard the Priscilla bound for Victoria, Australia, on 15 October 1852. [NRS.HD4/5]

BETHUNE, PETER, born 1830, from Uig, Skye, emigrated via Liverpool aboard the Priscilla bound for Victoria, Australia, on 15 October 1852. [NRS.HD4/5]

BETHUNE, RODERICK, born 1818, Sarah born 1816, Ann born 1841, Janet born 1843, Mary born 1846, and Malcolm born 1848, from Ulinish, Skye, emigrated via Glasgow on board the Georgiana bound to Port Philip, Australia, on 13 July 1852. [NRS.HD4/5]

BLACK, ANGUS, born 1781, in Fiart, Lismore, died 11 April 1847, husband of Eve Keith, born 1795, died 6 July 1877. [Lismore gravestone]

BLACK, JOHN, tailor on Lismore, [Liosmor], a petition, 1832. [NRS.GD170.564.25]

BLACK, MURDOCH, tenant of Aboss, Ulva, in 1824. [NRS.GD174.1140.9]

BLAIR, WILLIAM, born 13 January 1800, 'valued manager of James Forsyth Esq.', died at Glengorm on 1 June 1868. [Kilmore Dervaig gravestone, Mull]

BLUE, DUNCAN, born on Colonsay, [Colbhasa], in 1803, emigrated to Prince Edward Island in 1852, died 21 January 1881. [Little Sands gravestone, Prince Edward Island]

BONAR, DAVID, a tenant in Bowmore, [Bogha Mor], Islay, [Ile], 1844. [NRS.SC50.5.1844.62]

BROWN, JOHN, in Ardachy, Gigha, [Giogha], 1841. [NRS.SC50.5.1841.60]

BROWN, LEWIS, in Ardachyh, Gigha, [Giogha], 1841. [NRS.SC50.5.1841.60]

BROWNLIE, ANDREW, a linen weaver in Keills, [A'Chill], Islay, in 1828. [I.247]

BUCHANAN, ALEXANDER, born 1814, Catherine born 1814, Mary born 1835, John born 1837, Malcolm born 1841, Kate born 1846, Ann born 1849, and Christy an infant, emigrated via Liverpool aboard the Priscilla bound for Victoria on 15 October 1852. [NRS.HD4/5]

BUCHANAN, ANGUS, born 1828, Christy born 1824, Margaret born 1851, from Scorr, emigrated via Liverpool aboard the Araminta bound for Geelong, Australia, on 20 June 1852. [NRS.HD4/5]

BUCHANAN, CATHERINE, born 1808, Flora born 1833, Catherine born 1838, and Jane born 1840, from Garos, [Gearos], Skye, emigrated via Liverpool aboard the Allison bound for Melbourne on 13 September 1852. [NRS.HD4/5]

BUCHANAN, CATHERINE, born 1836, from Broadford, [An y-Ath Leathann], Skye, emigrated via Glasgow on board the Georgiana bound to Port Philip, Australia, on 13 July 1852. [NRS.HD4/5]

BUCHANAN, DONALD, born 1817, wife Ann Bethune born 1816, Janet born 1839, Marion born 1841, Catherine born 1843, and Ann born 1850, from Glen Halten, [Gleann Shealtainn], Skye, emigrated via Glasgow on board the Georgiana bound to Port Philip, Australia, on 13 July 1852. [NRS.HD4/5]

BUCHANAN, HUGH, born 1773, at Faolinmore, [An Fhaoilinn Mor], later in Torosay, died in May 1850, husband of Catherine McInnes, born 1777, died in November 1854. [Kilpatrick Duart gravestone, Torosay]

BUCHANAN, JANET, with children Duncan, Malcolm, and Alexander, from Skye aboard the Malay bound for Sydney, Nova Scotia, in 1830. [NSARM.RG1.67/19]

BUCHANAN, JOHN, born 1823, Mary born 1824, Donald born 1843, and Mary an infant, from Achnahanait, emigrated via Liverpool aboard the Priscilla bound for Victoria on 15 October 1852. [NRS.HD4/5]

BUCHANAN, JOHN, and sister, from Waterloo, Skye, applied to emigrate to Australia in 1854. [NRS.GD221.4437.1]

BUDGE, RANALD, and his sister in Portree, Skye, children of a crofter in Kilvaxter, [Cille Bhacastair], Skye, applied to emigrate to Australia in 1854. [NRS.GD221.4437.1]

BUDGE, WILLIAM, and his sister in Kilvaxter, Skye, applied to emigrate to Australia in 1854. [NRS.GD221.4437.1]

BURGESS, JOHN, a writer in Portree, [Port Righ], Skye, 1831. [NRS.CS46.1831.5.14]

CAMERON, ALLAN, on North Uist, [Uibhist], 1814.
[NRS.CC2.7.62.7]

CAMERON, ANGUS, tenant in Huistle, Skye, died in Bracadale,
Skye, on 29 July 1814, decreet dative, dated 10 May 1818.
[NRS.CC12.7.44.7]

CAMERON, ANNE, from Muck, emigrated via Fort William to
Quebec in 1802. [LAC.MG23.183]

CAMERON, DONALD, with Anne and children Anne, Charles
and Mary, from Skye aboard the Malay bound for Sydney,
Nova Scotia, in 1830. [NSARM.RG1.67/19]

CAMERON, DONALD, born 1791, with Catherine born 1819,
Christy born 1822, John born 1827, Ann born 1829, Ewen born
1836, Ann McLellan born 1844, and James McLellan born
1846, from North Uist, [Uibhist], emigrated via Greenock
aboard the Cashmere of Glasgow bound for Quebec in 1849.
[NRS.GD221.4011.53]

CAMERON, DONALD, born 1809, Susan born 1816, John born
1838, and Dugald born 1841, from Tobermory, [Tobar Mhoire],
Mull, emigrated via Liverpool aboard the Marmion bound for
Moreton Bay, Australia, on 28 August 1852. [NRS.HD4/5]

CAMERON, DUNCAN, in Portree, Skye, cash book, 1849.
[NRS.HD2.18]

CAMERON, EWAN, born 1797 on Skye, emigrated to Prince
Edward Island in 1829, died there on 28 April 1892. [St John's
gravestone, Belfast, PEI]

CAMERON, HUGH, a merchant in Tobermory, Mull, and his
trustees in 1837. [NRS.CS228.B18.31]

CAMERON, JEAN, born 1780 on Rum, emigrated via Leith on
board the St Lawrence of Newcastle bound for Port Hawkesby,
Cape Breton, in 1828. [PANS.M6.100]

CAMERON, JOHN, from Muck, emigrated via Fort William to Quebec in 1802. [LAC.MG23.183]

CAMERON, RANALD, with his wife, one son, and two daughters, from Achtalean, Skye, applied to emigrate to Australia in 1854. [NRS.GD221.1.4437.1]

CAMERON, ..., emigrated from Tobermory, Mull, on board the Monarch on 9 July 1823, landed in Quebec on 17 August 1823. [MH.23.8.1823]

CAMPBELL, ALEXANDER, born 1770, in Sorkamull, died 23 September 1847, husband of Mary MacArthur, born 1773, died 24 February 1847. [Glen Aros gravestone, Mull]

CAMPBELL, ALEXANDER, born 1786, a labourer from Mull, with sisters Mary born 1784, and Sarah born 1784, emigrated from Oban aboard the Clarendon of Hull, bound for Charlottetown, Prince Edward Island, in August 1808. [TNA.CO226.23]

CAMPBELL, ALEXANDER, from Islay, father of Polly, Catherine and Jean, in America by 1796. [NRS.CS17.1.15/182]

CAMPBELL, ALEXANDER, minister of Portree, Skye, died there, husband of Margaret McLeod, an edict of executry dated 22 March 1815. [NRS.CC12.7.43.1]

CAMPBELL, ALEXANDER, with Kate and children Anne, Kate, and Duncan, from Skye aboard the Malay bound for Sydney, Nova Scotia, in 1830. [NSARM.RG1.67/19]

CAMPBELL, ALEXANDER, with Christy and son John, from Skye aboard the Malay bound for Sydney, Nova Scotia, in 1830. [NSARM.RG1.67/19]

CAMPBELL, ALEXANDER, fourth son of the late Kenneth Campbell of Stroud, Harris, died in Montreal, Lower Canada, on 14 June 1854. [W.XV.1562]

CAMPBELL, Captain ANGUS, of Ensay, Harris, [Easaigh, na Hearadh], died on Harris in January 1812, edict of executry 1818. [NRS.CC12.5.4.4; CC12.7.44.8]

CAMPBELL, ANGUS, a tailor in Bahirva, Barra, [Barraigh], was accused of assaulting Christine McDonald at Brevig, Barra, in 1843. [NRS.AD14.43.18]

CAMPBELL, ANGUS, born 1814, with Marion born 1816, Christina born 1841, Murdoch born 1844, Duncan born 1846, Marion born 1849, and Duncan born 1857, emigrated from Harris [Na Hearadh], on board the Clansman bound for Australia on 13 July 1857. [NRS.GD371.241.1]

CAMPBELL, ARCHIBALD, a merchant in Scarinish, Tiree, [Sgairinis, Tiriodh], 22 October 1818. [NRS.CC12.2.14/2]

CAMPBELL, ARCHIBALD, tenant in Roskernie, Islay, 1818. [NRS.GD64.1.112]

CAMPBELL, ARCHIE, tenant of Lower Kilvickewan, [Cill Mhic Eoghainn], Ulva, [Ulbha], in 1824. [NRS.GD174.1140.9]

CAMPBELL, ARCHIE, tenant of Eolasary, Ulva, in 1824. [NRS.GD174.1140.9]

CAMPBELL, ARCHIBALD, born 1791, Port Charlotte, [Sgioba], Islay, accused of wounding in 1843. [NRS.AD14.43.366]

CAMPBELL, ARCHIBALD, born 1832, son of Colin Campbell and his wife Catherine Munro, died in Echuca, Australia, on 5 October 1867. [Kilchuimen gravestone, Islay]

CAMPBELL, Colonel CHARLES, of Barbreck, disposed of the lands of Ulva, Ormsaig, and Staffa, to Colin McDonald of Boisdale, South Uist, 1805-1803. [NRS.GD174.24.28]

CAMPBELL, COLIN, born 1785 in Mulindry, Islay, son of George Campbell and his wife Elizabeth Graham, emigrated to North Carolina in 1818, later moved to Upper Canada, in 1828. [SG]

CAMPBELL, COLIN, a merchant in Kilchoman, [Cill Chomain], Islay, an edict of executry, 9 January 1805. [NRS.CC12.3.7-34]

CAMPBELL, COLIN, born 1790, from Islay, emigrated to the Red River settlement in 1811. [PAC.M155.145]

CAMPBELL, COLIN, at Tapol later in Ormsaig, letters, 1820s. [NRS.GD174.255]

CAMPBELL, COLIN, of Duart, [Dubhaird], Mull, letters, 1826-1832. [NRS.GD174.1677/1829]

CAMPBELL, COLIN, born 1805, Ann born 1804, John born 1830, Donald born 1834, and Julia born 1838, from Renitra on the Ross of Mull, emigrated via Liverpool bound for Moreton Bay, Australia, in 1852. [NRS.HD.4/5]

CAMPBELL, COLIN, born 1803, Margaret born 1804, Mary born 1822, James born 1824, Rachel born 1830, John born 1832, Margaret born 1834, and Archibald born 1836, from Iona, [Eilean Idhe], emigrated via Liverpool aboard the Marmion bound for Moreton Bay, Australia, on 28 August 1852. [NRS.HD.4/5]

CAMPBELL, DONALD, born 1782, a labourer from Mull, with wife Ann born 1785, emigrated from Oban, [An t-Oban], aboard the Clarendon of Hull, bound for Charlottetown, Prince Edward Island, in August 1808. [TNA.CO226.23]

CAMPBELL, DONALD, late of Killandine, now at Breachacha, [Breac Achadh], Coll, and Jane Gregorson, a marriage contract dated 24 October 1824. [NRS.NRAS.1285, box 2/2]

CAMPBELL, DONALD, died 9 May 1841, husband of Elizabeth Harriet McLaine who died 4 April 1837, parents of Murdoch, died 30 October 1834, and Elizabeth Jarvis who died 23 January 1826. [Killean, [Cill Eathain], Loch Spelve gravestone, Mull]

CAMPBELL, DONALD, tenant of Ardellum, Ulva, [Ulbha], in 1824. [NRS.GD174.1140.9]

CAMPBELL, DONALD, born 1802, his wife born 1804, from Islay, emigrated via Glasgow on board the Damascus bound for Toronto, Canada, on 28 June 1862. [JRK]

CAMPBELL, DONALD, born 1806 on Tiree, [Tiriodh], emigrated to Cape Breton in 1831, died 27 January 1869. [Stewartdale Cemetery, Inverness County, Nova Scotia.]

CAMPBELL, DONALD, born 1802, Catherine born 1808, John born 1830, Mary born 1833, Anne born 1835, Christy born 1837, Ronald born 1839, Marion born 1847, Janet born 1849, from Borline, [Borlainn], Skye, emigrated via Liverpool aboard the Araminta bound for Geelong, Australia, on 20 June 1852. [NRS.HD4/5]

CAMPBELL, DONALD, born 1809, Mary born 1817, Rachel born 1836, Catherine born 1839, Marion born 1841, Margaret born 1843, Neil born 1845, Colin born 1847, Margaret born 1849, and Lexy born 1851, emigrated from Harris on board the Clansman bound for Australia on 13 July 1857. [NRS.GD371.241.1]

CAMPBELL, DONALD, minister of Ross, Mull, in 1843. [M.274]

CAMPBELL, DOUGAL, born 1800 on Islay, died 29 November 1834. [Old Scots gravestone, Charleston, South Carolina]

CAMPBELL, DUGALD, minister of Kilfinichen and Kilvicheon, Mull, in 1791. [M.348]; born 1750, 32 years a minister of Kilvickeon, died 21 April 1824, husband of Elizabeth Campbell, died 21 July 1856, parents of Donald born 1 November 1786, later minister at Kilvickeon, died in August 1855. [Kilvickeon, [Cill Mhic Eoghainn], gravestone, Mull]

CAMPBELL, DUNCAN, tacksman of Tresnish [Treisinis], at Kilmaluag, a letter, 1815. [M.195]

CAMPBELL, DUNCAN, born 1790 on Islay, emigrated to America in 1802, settled in Charleston, South Carolina, and later in Charlotte, Mecklenburg County, North Carolina, was naturalised in Mecklenburg on 10 May 1823. [NSCA.CR.065.311.1]

CAMPBELL, DUNCAN, born 1814, Mary born 1815, Mary born 1836, Ann born 1838, Hugh born 1840, Christy born 1844, Archibald born 1848, and Margaret born 1850, from Uig, emigrated via Liverpool aboard the Allison bound for Melbourne, Australia, in 1852. [NRS.HD4/5]

CAMPBELL, DUNCAN, born 1818, his wife born 1826, Dugald 54born 1850, Catherine born 1852, Margaret born 1854, Ann born 1855, Bella born 1858, Jessie born 1860, and Mary aged 6 months, from Islay, emigrated via Glasgow on board the Damascus bound for Toronto, Canada, on 28 June 1862. [JRK]

CAMPBELL, GEILLS, relict of Malcolm Campbell late of Barmulloch, residing in Balephetrish, [Baile Pheadrais], Tiree. 22 October 1818. [NRS.CC12.2.14]

CAMPBELL, GEORGE, tenant at the Sound of Ulva, 1824. [NRS.GD174.1140.9]

CAMPBELL, HESTER, born 1799, youngest daughter of Dugald Campbell minister of Kilvickeon, died 20 June 1847. [Kilvickeon gravestone, Mull]

CAMPBELL, JAMES, was accused of embezzlement at the Appin Slateworks on Lismore in 1845. [NRS.AD14.45.329]

CAMPBELL, JANET, born 1776, died 1 May 1828, mother of Donald Carmichael, born 1803, died 15 October 1828, in Balichdrach. [Glen Aros gravestone, Mull]

CAMPBELL, JOHN, born 1752, a labourer from Mull, with wife Isabel born 1753, and sons Roderick born 1778, Donald, on the Clarendon of Hull, bound for Charlottetown, Prince Edward Island, in August 1808. [TNA.CO226.23]

CAMPBELL, JOHN, Commander of the Customs cutter Prince of Wales at Scarsdale, Bowmore, Islay, testament, 25 August 1808, Comm. of the Isles. [NRS.CC12]

CAMPBELL, JOHN, born 1816, the younger of Possil, died 1885. [M.322/385]

CAMPBELL, JOHN, of Ardmore, Islay, born 1800, chamberlain of the Ross of Mull from 1846, died 1872. [M.349-357/446]

CAMPBELL, JOHN, born 1808 in Raag, Skye, a stonemason, husband of Ann McLean, emigrated to Canada before 1832. [SG]

CAMPBELL, JOHN, tenant in Tiree, a decreet dated 27 September 1821. [NRS.CS44.189.25]

CAMPBELL, JOHN, a joint-tenant of Auchenadeunie, Lismore, [Liosmor], a letter to Sir Duncan Campbell of Barcaldine, his landlord, re inability to pay rent, 1824. [NRS.GD170.2349]

CAMPBELL, JOHN, schoolmaster on Lismore, a letter, 1833. [NRS.GD170.2346]

CAMPBELL, JOHN, son of Ewen Campbell in Lower Bornish, South Uist, accused of housebreaking in 1836. [NRS.AD14.36.45]

CAMPBELL, JOHN, jr., in Chinquacousy, Canada, heir to his grandfather John Campbell, sr., in Glenmachry, Islay, who died in 1841. [NRS.SH.1872]

CAMPBELL, KENNETH, tacksman of Scalpa, [Sgalpaigh], Harris, died on 4 September 1807 on Harris, a deed, 1810. [NRS.CC12.7.40.6]

CAMPBELL, KENNETH, of Strond, [Srannda], Harris, died on Harris, spouse of Ann McLeod, edict of executry, 1817. [NRS.CC12.7.44.2]

CAMPBELL, LACHLAN, with family, from Cleadale, [Cleadail], Eigg, emigrated via Arisaig aboard The British Queen of Greenock to Quebec in 1790. [NAC.RG4A1.48.15874-5]

CAMPBELL, MALCOLM, of Barmulloch, residing in Balephetrish, Tiree, an edict of executry, dated 15 May 1816. [NRS.CC2.7.43.8]

CAMPBELL, MALCOLM, with his wife Anne, from Skye aboard the Malay bound for Sydney, Nova Scotia, in 1830. [NSARM.RG1.67/19]

CAMPBELL, MARGARET, and her husband Duncan McNab, on Taransay, [Tarasaigh], Harris, a decreet, 1819. [NRS.CS40.31.58]

CAMPBELL, MARGARET, only child of Angus Campbell of Ensay, [Easaigh], Harris, a decreet, 1819. [NRS.CS40.31.58]

CAMPBELL, MARION, third daughter of the late Malcolm Campbell of Cornaig, Coll, married John Campbell of Picton, Nova Scotia, on 31 January 1826. [SM.ns.18.510]

CAMPBELL, MARY, daughter of the deceased Kenneth Campbell tacksman of Scalpa, Harris, and her husband Kenneth McLeod, on Lewis, a decreet, 1819. [NRS.CS40.31.58]

CAMPBELL, MURDO, with his wife Anne, from Skye aboard the Malay bound for Sydney, Nova Scotia, in 1830. [NSARM.RG1.67/19]

CAMPBELL, MURDOCH, born 1805 on Uist, emigrated to Cape Breton in 1831, died 16 September 1878, husband of Mary McKinnon born 20 August 1812, died 11 April 1874. [Stewartdale Cemetery, Inverness County, Nova Scotia]

CAMPBELL, NEIL, born in South Uist in 1745, died at Balls Creek, Cape Breton, Nova Scotia, on 26 January 1843. [Halifax Times, 14.2.1743]

CAMPBELL, POLLY, eldest daughter of Alexander Campbell, from Islay, settled in America, married .... Mumford by 1800. [NRS.CS17.1.19.263]

CAMPBELL, RODERICK, son of John Campbell [1721 – 1805] and his wife Margaret McLeod, died in Jamaica. [Dunvegan gravestone, Skye]

CAMPBELL, WALTER FREDERICK, of Islay, born 1798, Member of Parliament for Argyll; 1848. [NRS.SC50.5.1848.5]; died 1855. [M.446]

CAMPBELL, Captain, in Quinish, [Cuidhinis], Mull, in 1843. [MS274]

CARMICHAEL, CHRISTIAN, wife of Dougal McIntyre on Lismore, emigrated to South Carolina around 1821, settled in Dillon, S.C. [SHC]

CARMICHAEL, DONALD, in Cattadale, [Catadal], Islay, 1818. [NRS.GD64.1.112]

CARMICHAEL, DONALD, born 1834, with his wife born 1831, from Islay, emigrated via Glasgow on board the Damascus bound for Toronto, Canada, on 28 June 1862. [JRK]

CARMICHAEL, DUGALD, in Nosebridge, Kilarrow, Islay, 1818. [NRS.GD64.1.112]

CARMICHAEL, DUGALD, a drover and cattle dealer on Islay, 1822. [NRS.CS233.Seqn.S.C.1.64]

CARMICHAEL, DUGALD, a joint-tenant of Auchenadeunie, Lismore, a letter to Sir Duncan Campbell of Barcaldine, his landlord, re inability to pay rent, 1824. [NRS.GD170.2349]

CARMICHAEL, JOHN, born 1808 on Tiree, died in April 1874, husband of Catherine McCallum, born 1810 on Tiree, died on 24 December 1897. [Little Narrows, Victoria County, Nova Scotia]

CARMICHAEL, JOHN, a joint-tenant of Auchenadeunie, Lismore, a letter to Sir Duncan Campbell of Barcaldine, his landlord, re inability to pay rent, 1824. [NRS.GD170.2349]

CARRICK, JANET, daughter of John Carrick a farmer on Islay, versus George Nimmo, a mason in Edinburgh, a Process of Divorce, 1801. [NRS.CC8.6.1100]

CARSTAIRS, JOHN, of Gigha, 1836. [NRS.CS46.1836.5/39]

CHIENE, GEORGE, factor at Eallabus, Islay, in 1838. [I.201]

CHISHOLM, RODERICK, on South Uist, a letter dated 18 March 1800. [NRS.NRAS.2177, bundle 1506]

CLARK, DONALD, born 1816 in Iona, residing in Glasgow, accused of housebreaking, 1834. [NRS.AD14.34.57]

CLARK, DUNCAN, born 1790, minister of Torosay, died 1878. [M.446]

CLARK, NEILL, a crofter at Drimiyeonbeg, Gigha, in 1850. [NRS.SC50.5.1850.10]

COLQUHOUN, DONALD, born 1814, at Kilpatrick, died 13 November 1847, brother of Angus Colquhoun tenant of Ardchoirk. [Kilpatrick [Cill Phadraig] Duart gravestone, Torosay]

COLQUHOUN, NEIL, with his wife, son, and two daughters, in Portree, Skye, applied to emigrate to Australia in 1854. [NRS.GD221.4437.1]

COLQUHOUN, PATRICK, in Gruinard, [Gruinneart], Islay, deceased, an inventory, 1822. [NRS.CS97.94C.16]

COLVILLE, JOHN, joint-tenant of Machrimore Mill, Mull, in 1838. [NRS.C50.5.1838.38]

COLVILLE, WILLIAM, joint-tenant of Machrimore Mill, Mull, in 1838. [NRS.C50.5.1838.38]

CONNELL, COLIN, born 1786, from Tobermory, Mull, aboard the brig Humphreys bound for Prince Edward Island in 1806. [PAPEI.2702]

COWAN, JOHN, a merchant in Tarbert, [An Tairbeart], Gigha, 18.. [NRS.CS2.9.68]

CRAWFORD, DAVID, in Bowmore, Islay, was accused of assault in 1817. [NRS.AD14.17.118]

CRAUFORD, ROBERT, a linen weaver in Keills, Islay, in 1828. [I.247]

CUMMING, MARY, born 1798, Archibald born 1823, and Kate born 1830, from Carbost, Burnisdale, Skye, emigrated via Liverpool aboard the Priscilla bound for Victoria in 1852. [NRS.HD4/5]

CUNNINGHAM, JOHN, smith at Killian, [Cill Eathain], Lismore, a petition, 1830. [NRS.GD170.564.20]

CURRIE, ALEXANDER, in Conispy, [Comhnaidh nan Easbaig], Bridgend, Kilchoman, Islay, was accused of murder in 1823. [NRS.AD14.23.42]

CURRIE, ALEXANDER, sometime of Berlie, later at Octofad, [An t-Ochdamh Fada], Islay, a petition, 1840. [NRS.SC50.5.1840.7]

CURRIE, DOMNHULL, born 1789, Catriona MacPherson his wife, Mor, Seumas, and Domnhull, from Bruernish, Barra, possibly emigrated on board the Harmony to Cape Breton in 1821.

CURRIE, DONALD, born 1799, in Conispy, Bridgend, Kilchoman, Islay, was accused of murder in 1823. [NRS.AD14.23.42]

CURRIE, HUGH, a whisky distiller at Octovullin, Islay, in 1801, and 1818. [NRS.JP36.5.46]

CURRIE, JOHN, a tenant of Garmony, Mull, was evicted in 1800. [M.283]

CURRIE, JOHN, emigrated aboard the Emperor Alexander of Aberdeen, master Alexander Watt, from Tobermory, Mull, to Sydney, Cape Breton, in July 1823., landed on 16 September 1823. [Inverness Journal, 30 January 1824]

CURRIE, JOHN, tenant of Ferinardry, Ulva, in 1824. [NRS.GD174.1140.9]

CURRIE, MALCOLM, a tenant of Garmony, Mull, was evicted in 1800. [M.283]

CURRIE, MARY, wife of Nicolas McCalman, a sailor in Bowmore, Islay, were accused of housebreaking in 1837. [NRS.AD14.37.194]

CUTHBERTSON, GEORGE, born 1741, in Tobermory, died 16 April 1818. [Tobermory gravestone]

CUTHBERTSON, ROBERT, an officer of the Herring Fishing in Tobermory, Mull, letters, 1825-1832. [NRS.GD174.1963][M.447]

DARROCH, ALEXANDER, of Ardfernal, Jura, [Aird Fhearnail, Diura], born 1806 on Jura, married Janet Shaw in 1828, emigrated to Cumberland County, North Carolina, in 1847. [NCSA.2.57]

DARROCH, ARCHIBALD, tenant of Aboss, Ulva, in 1824. [NRS.GD174.1140.9]

DARROCH, ARCHIBALD, found guilty of an assault in Lagg, [An Lag], Jura and Colonsay, was imprisoned for a month in 1829. [NRS.JC26.1829.437]

DARROCH, JOHN, tenant of Ballygartan, Ulva, in 1824. [NRS.GD174.1140.9]

DARROCH, NIEL, tenant of Glaknagallon, Ulva, in 1824. [NRS.GD174.1140.9]

DINGWALL, ALEXANDER, a servant in Lyndale, [Lianadail], Skye, 1812. [NRS.AD14.12.36]

DINGWALL, MARY, born 1813, a forger in Portree, Skye, in 1836. [NRS.AD14.36.40]

DOUGLAS, JAMES, a tenant in Bowmore, Islay, 1844. [NRS.SC50.5.1844.62]

DOUGLAS, ROBERT, born 1794 in Bowmore, Islay, emigrated via Belfast to America, was naturalised in New York on 31 March 1821. [NARA]

DRUMMOND, THOMAS, the procurator fiscal in Stornaway, [Steornabhagh], Lewis, in 1834, a letter. [NRS.46.4.268]

DUNCAN, ARCHIBALD, born 1797, a slate manufacturer on Lismore, accused of assault in 1835. [NRS.AD14.35.162]

ELLIOT, Captain, in Portree, Skye, a memorandum, 1847. [NRS.HD20.47]

FALCONER, HECTOR, and his wife Mary Ross, in Handa, [Eilean Shannda], were parents of Flory baptised there in 1830, and Catherine baptised there in 1832. [HS.20.5]

FARLAN, ARCHIBALD, born 1836, died in 1853. [Kilvickean gravestone, Mull]

FERGUSON, ALEXANDER, born 1790, a missionary at Salen, Ulva, and Kilfinchen, and from 1828 minister of Tobermory,

Mull, husband of Catherine Macdonald, he died 4 June 1853. [M.304][Tobermory gravestone]

FERGUSON, CHRISTY, born 1799, with Donald Mathieson born 1828, and John Mathieson born 1831, from North Uist, emigrated via Greenock aboard the Waterhen of London bound for Quebec in 1849. [NRS.GD221.4435]

FERGUSON, DONALD, of Penny Loden, Benbecula, [Beinn a'Bhaoghla], an edict of executry 1815. [NRS.CC12.7.43.3]

FERGUSON, DUNCAN, minister to a Baptist congregation on the Ross of Mull around 1850. [M.349]

FERGUSON, HECTOR, born 1817, Mary born 1830, from St Kilda, [Hiort], emigrated via Liverpool aboard the Priscilla bound for Victoria on 15 October 1852. [NRS.HD4/5]

FERGUSON, JOHN, tenant of Culinish, Ulva, in 1824. [NRS.GD174.1140.9]

FERGUSON, MARY, born 1829, from North Uist, emigrated via Greenock aboard the Cashmere of Glasgow bound for Quebec in 1849. [NRS.GD221.4011.53]

FERGUSON, MALCOLM, born 1821, wife Catherine born 1829, and daughter Mary born 1849, from St Kilda, [Hiorta], emigrated aboard the Priscilla to Victoria in 1852. [NRS.HD4/5]

FERGUSON, NIELL, born 1771, shoemaker in Penmore, [Am Peighinn Mor], died 8 January 1837. [Calgary gravestone, Mull]

FERGUSON, RODERWICK, in Dunvegan, Skye, 1821. [NRS.CS234.seqn., F2.14]

FINLAYSON, ALEXANDER, with Christy and children Angus, Christy, and Anne, from Skye aboard the Malay bound for Sydney, Nova Scotia, in 1830. [NSARM.RG1.67/19]

FINLAYSON, MURDOCH, born 1813, Catherine born 1816, and Malcolm born 1835, from Balmeanoch, [Am Baile Meadhanach], Skye, emigrated via Liverpool aboard the Priscilla bound for Victoria on 15 October 1852. [NRS.HD4/5]

FLETCHER, HUGH, born 1785, farmer in Tirghoil, died 22 April 1847. [Kilpatrick gravestone, Mull]

FLETCHER, HUGH, with his wife Catherine MacLean, and nine children, in Tirghoil, Mull, emigrated to Canada in the 1850s. [M.356]

FLETCHER, JAMES, at Ferry Glebe, Gigha, in 1850. [NRS.SC50.5.1850.10]

FLETCHER, JOHN, sr., a tenant of Ledirkle, Mull, was evicted in 1800. [M.283]

FLETCHER, JOHN, jr., a tenant of Ledirkle, Mull, was evicted in 1800. [M.283]

FORSYTH, JAMES, of Glengorm, born 15 August 1801 in Jamaica, died at Glengorm on 24 February 1862, husband of Maria Magdalena, born 28 February 1808, died 27 May 1890. [Kilmore Dervaig gravestone, Mull]

FRASER, ALEXANDER, born 1757 on Sleat, [Sleite], died in South Carolina on 21 September 1830, his wife Mary, born 1766 on Sleat, died 22 August 1822, both buried in the Scotch Cemetery, Bethune, Kershaw County, S.C. [Bethune gravestone]

FRASER, WILLIAM, was 'drowned in going to Eigg' a letter of 1817. [NRS.GD243.4.11]

FRASER, WILLIAM, born 1759 on Sleat, died in South Carolina on 21 October 1832, buried in the Scotch Cemetery, Bethune, Kershaw County, S.C. [Bethune gravestone]

GALBREATH, ADAM, tacksman of Ardminish, [Aird Mheanais], Gigha, Giogha], 1848. [NRS.SC50.5.1848.32]

GALBRAITH, DONALD, son of John Galbraith a farmer at Drummyconbeg, Gigha, was accused of assault in 1831. [NRS.JC13.70]

GALBREATH, JOHN, farmer at Drimadiro, Gigha, in 1850. [NRS.SC50.5.1850.10]

GALBREATH, MALCOLM, tenant in Keills, [A'Chill], Gigha, 1839. [NRS.SC50.1839.18]

GALBREATH, NEIL, at New Quay, Gigha, in 1849. [NRS.SC50.5.1849.3]

GALBREATH, PETER, tacksman of Ardminish, Gigha, 1848. [NRS.SC50.5.1848.32]

GIBBONS, EDWARD, in Fearlick, [Feoirlig], Dunvegan, Skye, victim of a crime in 1837. [NRS.AD14.37.35]

GILCHRIST, ALEXANDER, on Islay, 1830. Sequestration. [NRS.CS236.628.11]

GILLIES, ANGUS, born 1754, resident in Tobermory, died 28 February 1803, husband of Isobel McLaren McLean, born 1757, died 16 March 1842.

GILLES, ANGUS, with Flora, from Skye aboard the Malay bound for Sydney, Nova Scotia, in 1830. [NSARM.RG1.67/19]

GILLES, ARCHIBALD, with wife Kate, and children Murdo, Margaret, and Angus, from Skye aboard the Malay bound for Sydney, Nova Scotia, in 1830. [NSARM.RG1.67/19]

GILLIES, DONALD, and his sister from Grealine, [Grealainn], Skye, emigrated to Australia aboard the Hornet in 1854. [NRS.GD221.443.7.1]

GILLIS, EOGHANN, with Ciorsdan MacMullin, from Bruernish, Barra, possibly emigrated on board the Harmony to Cape Breton in 1821.

GILLIES, EWAN, born 1825, Margaret born 1824, and Mary born 1851, from St Kilda, emigrated via Liverpool aboard the Priscilla bound for Victoria on 15 October 1852. [NRS.HD4/5]

GILLIES, JAMES, gardener at Lochbuy House, Mull, in 1812. [M.219]

GILLES, JOHN, with Flora and children Sarah, Duncan, Mary, Archibald, and Christy, from Skye aboard the Malay bound for Sydney, Nova Scotia, in 1830. [NSARM.RG1.67/19]

GILLES, JOHN, with Janet and son John, from Skye aboard the Malay bound for Sydney, Nova Scotia, in 1830. [NSARM.RG1.67/19]

GILLIS, LAWRENCE, born 1823 on Barra, emigrated to Nova Scotia in 1833, died 13 February 1912. [St Andrews RC Cemetery, Boisdale, Cape Breton].

GILLIS, MURCHADH, with his wife Catherine MacDonald, and daughter Seonaid, from the Kykes of Barra on the west side of Eriskay, possibly emigrated on board the Harmony to Cape Breton in 1821.

GILLES, MURDO, with his wife Margaret, and children Christy, Angus, Malcolm, James, Donald, and Susan, from Skye aboard the Malay bound for Sydney, Nova Scotia, in 1830. [NSARM.RG1.67/19]

GILLIES, MURDOCH, born 1809, a labourer from Skye, residing in Cliad, Tiree and Coll, 1832. [NRS.AD14.32.58]

GORDON, ALEXANDER, born 1805, Mary born 1806, Christy born 1836, Peter born 1839, and Margaret born 1843, from Eyre, Skye, emigrated via Liverpool aboard the Allison bound for Melbourne on 13 September 1852. [NRS.HD4/5]

GRAHAM, ALEXANDER, born 1758, died 22 October 1828, husband of Margaret Campbell, born 1775, died 27 January 1846, parents of John, born 1795, late in Jamaica, died 22 July 1827, and James, a merchant in Tobermory. [Tobermory gravestone]

GRAHAME, ALEXANDER, tacksman of Ballivicar, [Baile a'Bhiocaire], Kildalton, Islay, a petition re the late Marion McDuffie, spouse of Alexander Grahame tacksman of Ballivicar, 1800. [NRS.CC12.6.7.1]

GRAHAM, ARCHIBALD, at New Quay, Gigha, in 1849. [NRS.SC50.5.1849.3]

GRAHAM, or MACNEILL, CATHERINE, a widow in Cnochnanerdach, Gigha, 1841. [NRS.SC50.5.1841.60]

GRAHAM, JOHN, in Scarbreck farm, in Portree, Skye, accused of theft, 6 April 1801. [NRS.AC26.1801.1]

GRAHAM, JOHN, born 1819, Flora born 1822, Neil born 1851, from Harripool, [Harrapol], Skye, emigrated via Liverpool aboard the Araminta bound for Geelong, Australia, on 20 May 1852. [NRS.HD4/5]

GRAHAM, MARGARET, born 1808, died 12 October 1826. [Kilpatrick gravestone, Mull]

GRAHAM, MARY, born 1834, from Duntolin, emigrated via Liverpool aboard the Alison bound for Melbourne on 13 September 1852. [NRS.HD4/5]

GRANT, DONALD, in Ullinish, [Uilinis], Bracadale, Skye, letter re a liquor licence, 1807. [NRS.GD23.6.435]

GRANT, LACHLAN, born 1818, Flora born 1820, Donald born 1850, and Mary born 1852, from Sconser, [Sgonnsar], Skye, emigrated via Liverpool aboard the Araminta bound for Geelong, Australia, on 20 June 1852. [NRS.HD4/5]

GRANT, THOMAS, in Lagg, Jura and Colonsay, was victim of an assault, trial held in 1829. [NRS.JC26.1829.437]

GREGORSON, ANGUS, of Ardtornish, died in 1811, husband of Elizabeth Campbell of Achnaba, died 1819, parents of John born 5 April 1775, died 14 February 1846. [Lismore gravestone]

GREGORSON, ANGUS, born 1816, son of Donald Gregorson of Ardtonish, and his wife Phoebe MacLaine, a banker and lawyer in Oban became factor of the Lochbuy estate on Mull in 1837, died 1873. [M.448]

GREGORSON, JOHN, born 1775, in Ardtonish, [Aird Toirinis], Mull, letters, 1816-1840. [NRS.GD174.1638], Sheriff of Mull and Morvern, died 1846. [M.448]

HALL, THOMAS, a wright and undertaker in Portree, Skye, accused of theft, 6 April 1801. [NRS.AC26.1801.1]

HAMILTON, PATRICK, a linen weaver in Keills, Islay, in 1828. [I.247]

HENDERSON, ALLAN, in Dervaig, husband of Catherine Carmichael born 1767, died 26 June 1825. [Kilmore Dervaig gravestone, Mull]

HENDERSON, ARCHIBALD, tenant in West Tarbert, Gigha, 1839. [NRS.SC50.1839.18]

HENDERSON, DONALD, on Gigha in 1838. [NRS.SC50.5.1838.12]

HENDERSON, DUNCAN, born 1759, Sarah born 1759, Mary born 1786, Donald born 1788, Ann born 1792, and John born 1804, from Tobermory, Mull, aboard the brig Humphreys bound for Prince Edward Island in 1806. [PAPEI.2702]

HENDERSON, DUNCAN, a travelling merchant in Tobermory, Mull, was tried for assault in 1826. [NRS.JC26.1826.203]

HENDERSON, HUGH, on Gigha in 1838. [NRS.SC50.5.1838.12]

HILL, JOHN, merchant in Port Askaig, [Port Ascaig], Islay, an edict of executry, 1820. [NRS.CC12.7.45.1]

HOGG, SAMUEL, a manufacturer in Portree, Skye, records, 1849. [NRS.HD20.22]

HUME, ALEXANDER, of Harris, a memorial, 1807. [NRS.CS234.H9.9]

HUNTER, ALEXANDER, born 1784, from Tobermory, Mull, 1806. [PAPEI.2702]

JOHNSON, JOHN, a whisky distiller at Lagavulin, Islay, in 1818.

JOHNSTON, DONALD and JOHN, whisky distillers at Tallant, Islay, in 1801, later in 1818. [NRS.JP36.5.46]

JOHNSTON, DUNCAN, a whisky distiller in Tallant, Islay, in 1801. [NRS.JP36.5.46]

JOHNSTON, JOHN, a farmer from Craighouse, [Taigh na Creige], Jura, applied to emigrate to Canada in 1815. [TNA.CO385.2]

JOHNSTON, RUARAIDH, his wife Sarah [ex MacVicar] Shaw, Iain born 1803, Mairaid, Flora, and Ruaraidh born 1813, from Barra, emigrated on board the Harmony to Cape Breton in 1821.

KEITH, DUNCAN, in Port Ramsay, [Port Ramasaigh], Lismore, was accused of theft in 1818. [NRS.AD14.18.254]

KEITH, GEORGE, son of William Keith and his wife Elizabeth Cameron on Skye, emigrated to New York in 1803. [CS.265]

KEITH, HUGH, born 1772, son of William Keith and his wife Elizabeth Cameron on Skye, emigrated to North Carolina in 1803, settled in Crane's Creek, Moore County, N.C., died 1860. [CS.265]

KEITH, JAMES, son of William Keith and his wife Elizabeth Cameron on Skye, emigrated to North Carolina in 1803. [CS.265]

KEITH, JOHN, born on Islay around 1812, died in Keyser, North Carolina, on 10 November 1882. [Bethesda Cemetery, Aberdeen, Moore County, N.C.]

KEITH, NEIL, in Port Ramsay, Lismore, was accused of theft in 1818. [NRS.AD14.18.254]

KEITH, PEGGY, daughter of William Keith and his wife Elizabeth Cameron on Skye, emigrated to North Carolina in 1803, married John McDougald. [CS.265]

KELLY, DANIEL, born 1725 on Sleat, emigrated to Moore County, North Carolina, in 1803, with children Barbara, [1767-1849], Daniel, [1770-1829], James, [1772-1825], Donald, [1773-1855], John, [1778-1836], Peter, [1780-1853], Nancy, [1782-], Hugh, [1784-1851], and John Bethune, [1789-1847]. [CS.256]

KELLY, JOHN, born 1788 on Sleat, husband of Catherine Chisholm, died 25 August 1836. [Stewartsville gravestone, Laurenburg, Scotland County, North Carolina]

KELLY, JOHN, born 1789, died 9 February 1847. [Union Presbyterian gravestone, Moore County, North Carolina]

KELLY, NANCY, born 15 February 1784, died in North Carolina on 17 December 1858. [Kelly gravestone, Moore County, N.C.]

KELLY, PETER, born 1783, a farmer, emigrated to North Carolina in 1803, died 30 June 1853 in Moore County, North Carolina. [Union Presbyterian gravestone, Carthage, Moore County, N.C.]

KERR, CATHEL, and his wife Ann McLeod, in Handa, [Eilean Shannda], were parents of George baptised there in 1831. [HS.20.5]

LAMONT, ALLAN, born 1793, son of Malcolm Lamont in Killean, husband of Mary MacDougall, born 1798, former schoolmaster at Lochdon, former postmaster at Achnacrag, and former session clerk of Craigmure church, emigrated to Canada in 1851, settled at Grey Township, Canada West, a letter dated 9 August 1853, died in 1865, his children Allan, Archibald, Catherine, Dugald, Hugh, Malcolm, and Mary, also went to Canada, while Donald, Neil, and Marion remained in Scotland . [M.401-403/405]

LAMONT, ANGUS, born 1771, son of Donald Lamont and his wife Effy Black, in Ulva, later a tenant in Iona, died 1856, father of Mary born 1810, died 1893. [M.405]

LAMONT, ARCHIBALD, tenant of Lower Kilvickewan, Ulva, in 1824. [NRS.GD174.1140.9]

LAMONT, DONALD, tenant of Soriby, [Soiribidh], Ulva, in 1824. [NRS.GD174.1140.9]

LAMOND, DONALD, and his wife Barbara Falconer, on Handa, [Eilean Shannda], were parents of James baptised there in 1828, Williamina baptised there in 1829, John baptised there in 1831, and Barbara baptised there in 1832. [HS.20.5]

LAMONT, JOHN, tenant of Lower Kilvickewan, Ulva, in 1824. [NRS.GD174.1140.9]

LAMONT, JOHN, in Killocheon, Kilninian, [Cill Naoi Nighean], Ulva, victim of a crime aboard a steamboat, 1829. [NRS.AD14.29.98]

LAMONT, ROBERT, tenant of Ballygartan and Sorisby, Ulva, in 1824, [NRS.GD174.1140.9]; victim of a crime aboard a steamboat, 1829. [NRS.AD14.29.98]

LAMONT, SAMUEL, a millwright from Bowmore, Islay, emigrated aboard the Prince of Wales bound for the Red River Settlement in 1813. [PAC.M155,165-168]

LAYTON, Captan H., in Tobermory, Mull, letters, 1846-1847. [NRS.HD7.1]

LINDSAY, ALEXANDER, was found guilty of an assault in Lagg, Jura and Colonsay, was outlawed but absconded in 1829. [NRS.JC26.1829.437]

LINDSAY, JOHN, was found guilty of an assault in Lagg, Jura and Colonsay, was outlawed but absconded in 1829. [NRS.JC26.1829.437]

LINDSAY, NEIL, was found guilty of an assault in Lagg, Jura and Colonsay, was outlawed but absconded in 1829. [NRS.JC26.1829.437]

LIVINGSTON, ANGUS, born 1810, died in June 1882, husband of Ann McDougall, born 1818, died in May 1900. [Killean, Loch Spelve gravestone, Mull]

LIVINGSTON, ARCHIBALD, died 1842, husband of Elizabeth Paterson, died 10 October 1881. [Tobermory gravestone]

LIVINGSTONE, JOHN, in Portree, Skye, a letter dated 13 February 1804. [NRS.NRAS.3273/4289]

LIVINGSTON, JOHN, born 1786, from Tobermory, Mull, aboard the brig Humphreys bound for Prince Edward Island in 1806. [PAPEI.2702]

LIVINGSTON, MARY, born 1800 on the Ross of Mull, settled in Caledon, Peel County, Ontario, widow of Donald McEachen, died 14 February 1842. [Caledon gravestone]

MCALISTER, ALEXANDER, born in 1801, son of Duncan McAlister tenant in Portnahoven, [Port na h-Abhainne], Islay, was accused of plundering a wreck, in 1821. [NRS.AD14.21.166]

MCALISTER DANIEL, son of Duncan McAlister tenant in Portnahoven, Islay, was accused of plundering a wreck, in 1821. [NRS.AD14.21.166]

MACALISTER, Mrs MARY, born 1793, wife of John MacAlister of Strathaird, [Srath na h-Airde], Skye, died in Rome on 27 January 1869. [Protestant Cemetery gravestone, Rome]

MCALISTER, NORMAN, born in Skerrinish, [Sgeirinis], Skye, son of Ranald McAlister and his wife Anne McDonald, a Brevet Major of the Bengal Artillery, died in 1810. [BA.3.105]

MACALISTER, RANALD, third son of Dr MacAlister of Strathaird, Skye, died in Demerara on 31 March 1820. [BM.7.583]

MCALPINE, CATHERINE, a tenant in Bowmore, Islay, 1844. [NRS.SC50.5.1844.62]

MACALPINE, NEIL, schoolmaster of Ballygrant, Islay, in 1820s, author of a Gaelic-English Dictionary in 1834. [I.186]

MCARTHUR, ALEXANDER, of Ardmeanach, [1800-1850s]. [M354]

MCARTHUR, ALEXANDER, a crofter in Gortacofan, Bowmore, Islay, accused of assault in 1815. [NRS.AD14.15.118]

MCARTHUR, ALLAN, born 1767 on Canna, with his wife Catherine McDonald, born 1792 on Arran, and children Mary born 1817 on Canna, and Archibald born 1821 on Canna, emigrated to Nova Scotia in 1827. [Pond Road Cemetery, Sydney Mines, Cape Breton]; Allan died at Sydney Mines, Nova Scotia, on 18 May 1869. [McArthur gravestone, Cape Breton.]

MCARTHUR, ALLAN, was accused of sheep stealing on Staffa in 1831. [NRS.AD14.31.195]

MCARTHUR, ARCHIBALD, a tenant of Ormaig, Ulva, in 1824. [NRS.GD174.1087.1]

MCARTHUR, ARCHIBALD, tenant of Soriby, Ulva, in 1824. [NRS.GD174.1140.9]

MCARTHUR, ARCHIBALD, born 18 December 1821 on Canna, died at Sydney Mines, Cape Breton, on 18 May 1869. [McArthur gravestone, Cape Breton]

MCARTHUR, CHARLES, born 1807, son of Archibald McArthur tenant in Ormaig, died on 1 March 1825. [Kilviceuen gravestone, Ulva]

MCARTHUR, CHARLES, born 1822, his wife born 1826, Donald born 1853, John born 1858, Neil born 1860, and Ann born 1862, from Upper Killean, parish of Oa, [Obha],Islay, emigrated via Glasgow aboard the Damascus bound for Toronto on 28 June 1862. [JRK]

MCARTHUR, DONALD, tenant of Berniss, Ulva, in 1824. [NRS.GD174.1140.9]

MCARTHUR, FARQUHAR, tenant of Soriby, Ulva, in 1824. [NRS.GD174.1140.9]

MCARTHUR, FLORA, in Bowmore, Islay, last will and testament, 1814. [NRS.GD64.1.205]

MCARTHUR, HUGH, died in 1855. [Kilvickeon gravestone, Mull]

MACARTHUR, JOHN, drowned on the voyage of the Batavia on 16 June 1846. [Kilvickeon gravestone, Mull]

MCARTHUR, MALCOLM, tenant of Berniss, Ulva, in 1824. [NRS.GD174.1140.9]

MCARTHUR, NIEL, tenant of Soriby, Ulva, in 1824. [NRS.GD174.1140.9]

MCARTHUR, PATRICK, born 1740, minister of Torosay from 1779 until 1790 when he drowned in the Sound of Mull. [M.323/449]

MCARTHUR, PETER, born 1807, Isabella born 1812, John born 1833, Anne born 1831, Archibald born 1835, Dugald born 1837, Christianna born 1840, Flora born 1841, Donald born 1844, Mary born 1846, Eliza born 1848, and James born 1850, from Renitra on the Ross of Mull, emigrated via Liverpool aboard the Marmion bound for Moreton Bay, Australia, on 28 August 1852. [NRS.HD4/5]

MCARTHUR, Dr, in Kilninian, Mull, in 1843. [M.274]

MCARTIN, DUNCAN, born 1802 on Jura, emigrated to America in 1847, settled in Cumberland County, North Carolina, died in Moore County, N.C., on 13 March 1858. [NCPresbyterian.21.5.1868]

MCCASKILL, ALEXANDER, born 1804 in Minginish, Skye, died 24 March 1824 in South Carolina. [Scotch Cemetery gravestone, Bethune, Kershaw County, S.C]

MACASKILL, Captain ALLAN, born 1765, son of Reverend Malcolm MacAskill minister of the Small Isles and his wife Mary McLean of Coll, proprietor of Calgary, Mornish, Mull, died on 6 June 1828. [M.222/449]

MCCASKILL, ANGUS ALEXANDER, born 1769 on Skye, settled in North Carolina before 1806, died in Moore County, North Carolina, on 14 March 1807. [Old Scotch gravestone, Carthage, Moore County, N.C., gravestone]

MCASKILL, ARCHIBALD, born 1832, from North Uist, emigrated via Greenock aboard the Waterhen of London bound for Quebec in 1849. [NRS.GD221.4435]

MCCASKILL, DANIEL, born 1808 in Minginish, Skye, died 18 July 1842 in South Carolina. [Scotch Cemetery gravestone, Bethune, Kershaw County, S.C]

MCASKILL, DONALD, born 1807, Marion born 1812, Duncan born 1834, John born 1837, Kenneth born 1838, Peter born 1841, John born 1842, Ewan born 1845, and Donald born 1849, from Borline, [Borlainn], Skye, emigrated via Liverpool aboard the Araminta bound for Geelong, Australia, on 20 June 1852. [NRS.HD.4/5]

MCASKILL, HECTOR, born 1790 on Skye, married Christian Chisholm, emigrated to North Carolina, [NCSA.2.77]

MCASKILL, HUGH, [1799-1863], in Tallisker, Skye, a letter from John Tolmie in Uiginish, Skye, in 1844. [NRS.GD403.78][M.449]

MCCASKILL, JOHN, born 1812, Catherine born 1826, Mary born 1845, John born 1848, and Catherine born 1850, from Strathaird, [Srath na h-Airde], Skye, emigrated via Liverpool aboard the Priscilla bound for Victoria, Australia, on 15 October 1852. [NRS.HD4/5]

MCCASKILL, JOHN, born 1790 in Minginish, Skye, died in South Carolina on 16 August 1822, buried in the Scotch Cemetery, Bethune, Kershaw, S.C. [Bethune gravestone]

MCCASKILL, KENNETH, born 1800 in Minginish, Skye, died 18 April 1878 in South Carolina. [Scotch Cemetery gravestone, Bethune, Kershaw County, S.C]

MCCASKILL, MARION, born 1824, from Horneval, Skye, emigrated via Liverpool aboard the Allison bound for Melbourne on 13 September 1852. [NRS.HD4/5]

MCCASKILL, RACHEL, born 1839, from Portree, Skye, emigrated via Liverpool aboard the Priscilla bound for Victoria on 15 October 1852. [NRS.HD4/5]

MCASKILL, Dr, on Eigg in 1814. [NRS.CC2.7.62.7]; was 'drowned in going to Eigg' a letter, 1817. [NRS.GD243.4.11]

MCAULAY, AENEAS, born on Skye or Lewis, graduated from the University of Glasgow, chaplain to the West India Regiment, emigrated to Prince Edward Island aboard the Polly in 1803, Speaker of the PEI Provincial House in 1818, husband of Mary, daughter of Captain Samuel MacDonald of Sartle in Skye. [SP]

MCAULAY, ANGUS, born 1797, Anne born 1805, Donald born 1832, Ann born 1828, Flora born 1830, Kate born 1838, Marion born 1834, and Donald born 1851, from Kildonnan, Eigg, emigrated via Liverpool aboard the Priscilla bound for Victoria on 15 October 1852. [NRS.HD4/5]

MCAULAY, ARCHIBALD, born 1814, from North Uist, with Catherine born 1821, and Margaret born 1847, emigrated via Greenock aboard the Waterhen of London bound for Quebec in 1849. [NRS.GD221.4435]

MCAULAY, DONALD, a smith from Frobost, South Uist, with family, emigrated via Arasaig aboard The British Queen of Greenock to Quebec in 1790. [NAC.RG4A1.48.15874-5]

MCAULAY, DONALD, born 1797 on Lewis, settled in Nova Scotia, died 1884. [Little Narrows gravestone, Victoria County, Nova Scotia]

MCAULAY, GEORGE, born on Lewis, a merchant in Charleston, South Carolina, died 8 May 1826. [Old Scots gravestone, Charleston]

MCAULAY, GILBERT, born 1799, a fisherman in Portnahoven, [Port na h-Abhainne], Islay, was accused of plundering a wreck, in 1821. [NRS.AD14.21.166]

MCAULAY, JOHN, a servant from Frobost, South Uist, emigrated via Arisaig aboard The British Queen of Greenock to Quebec in 1790. [NAC.RG4A1.48.15874-5]

MCAULAY, JOHN, of Bosta Island, Bernera, Lewis, was accused of sheep stealing in 1837. [NRS.AD14.37.6]

MCAULAY, MALCOLM, born 1832, residing in Struary, Skye, with Christy born 1833, and Ann born 1826, emigrated via Glasgow aboard the Georgiana bound for Port Philip, Australia, on 13 July 1852. [NRS.HD4/5]

MCAULAY, MURDOCH, born on Lewis in 1791, died 20 August 1872. [Little Narrows gravestone, Victoria County, Nova Scotia]

MCAULAY, NORMAN, born on Lewis in 1812, emigrated to Nova Scotia in 1827, died 19 November 1899. [Little Narrows gravestone, Victoria County, Nova Scotia]

MCAULAY, SAMUEL, born 1828, residing in Glen Skeabost, Skye, with his wife Christy born 1831, and sisters Ann McAulay born 1832, and Christy, emigrated via Glasgow aboard the Georgiana bound for Port Philip, Australia, on 13 July 1852. [NRS.HD4/5]

MACCAIG, ALEXANDER, in Nosebridge, Islay, 1818. [NRS.GD64.1.112]

MCCAIG, DUNCAN, born 1756, farmer at Balgarve, Lismore, died at Clachan in 1846, husband of [1] Catherine Livingstone, and [2] Ann Stewart. [Lismore gravestone]

MCCAIG, MALCOLM, born 1786, merchant and farmer at Clachan, Lismore, died in April 1834, husband of Margaret Stewart, born 1797, died 2 August 1865. [Lismore gravestone]

MCCALL, ARCHIBALD, minister of Tiree, an edict of executry dated 15 January 1816. [NRS.CC12.7.43.9]; Archibald McCall minister of Tiree, deceased, husband of Flora McDougall, an edict of curator re their children Catherine, Isabella, Flora, Ann, and Donald, dated 27 April 1817. [NRS.SC54.6.4.3.8]

MCCALL, DONALD, a joint-tenant of Auchenadeunie, Lismore, a letter to Sir Duncan Campbell of Barcaldine, his landlord, re inability to pay rent, 1824. [NRS.GD170.2349]

MCCALL, JOHN, a joint-tenant of Auchenadeunie, Lismore, a letter to Sir Duncan Campbell of Barcaldine, his landlord, re inability to pay rent, 1824. [NRS.GD170.2349]

MACCALLUM, ALEXANDER, born 1774, tacksman of Ledmore, died 31 December 1833. [Glen Aros gravestone, Mull]

MCCALLUM, CHARLES, a tenant of Cragaig, Ulva, in 1824. [NRS.GD174.1087.1]

MCCALLUM, DONALD, a tenant of Cragaig, Ulva, in 1824. [NRS.GD174.1087.1]

MCCALLUM, JOHN, [1793-1836], a carpenter in Tobermory, Mull, 1823. [M.398]

MACCALLUM, JOHN, [1822-1909], a writer in Tobermory, [M.449]

MCCALLUM, LACHLAN, born 1752, miller at Gragaig, died on 2 February 1822. [Calgary Bay gravestone, Mull]

MCCALLUM, MALCOLM, a fisherman in Tiree, later in Campbeltown, 1849. [NRS.SC50.5.1849.12]

MCCALLUM, NEIL, a whisky distiller in Scarrabus, Islay, in 1801. [NRS.JP36.5.46]

MCCALLUM, NEIL, born 1776, a labourer from Mull, with wife Mary born 1776, and children John born 1796, Finlay born 1803, Archibald born 1803, Mary born 1805, and Donald born 1807, emigrated from Oban aboard the Clarendon of Hull, bound for Charlottetown, Prince Edward Island, in August 1808. [TNA.CO226.23]

MCCALLUM, NEIL, a whisky distiller at Ballygrant, Islay, in 1818.

MCCOLL, ARCHIBALD, [1746-1814], minister of Tiree. [M.325/449]

MCCOLL, DOUGALD, a teacher in Tobermory, Mull, in 1843. [M.274]

MCCOLL, DUGALD, a smith in Kilerne, Lismore, a letter, 1814. [NRS.GD170.2528]

MCCOLL, DUNCAN, born 1810, surgeon on Torosay, Mull, died 25 October 1882. [Lismore gravestone]

MCCOLL, DUNCAN, vintner in Clachan, Lismore, accused of assault in 1844. [NRS.AD14.44.111]

MCCOLL, Dr HECTOR, born 1799 at Ledmore, a surgeon in Tobermory, Mull, in 1843, died in 1891. [M.274/323]

MCCOLL, MALCOLM, a tenant on Lismore, a petition, 1830. [NRS.GD170.564.21]

MCCOLL, SAMUEL, in Auchasregan, Lismore, accused of theft in 1824. [NRS.AD14.24.266]

MCCOLMAN, NICHOL, born 1807, a shoemaker in Bowmore, Islay, was accused of theft from Neill Ferguson of Claddoch Farm, Kilchoman, Islay, in 1829. [NRS.AD14.29.316]

MACCONACHY, ARCHIBALD, tenant of Achamore, Gigha, 1839. [NRS.SC50.1839.18]

MCCONACHIE, DONALD, in Ardelamy, Gigha, 1841. [NRS.SC50.841.59]

MCCORE, ALEXANDER, a crofter in Nerrabus, Islay, was accused of deforcement in 1819. [NRS.AD14.19.27]

MCCORMICK, ALEXANDER, born 1842, from Islay emigrated via Glasgow aboard the Damascus bound for Toronto on 28 June 1862. [JRK]

MCCORMICK, DONALD, from Cleadale, Eigg, with family, emigrated via Arisaig aboard The British Queen of Greenock to Quebec in 1790. [NAC.RG4A1.48.15874-5]

MCCORMICK, JOHN, born 1785, SSPCK schoolmaster at Creich, Mull, in 1843, husband of Mary McDonald, died 1879. [M.450]

MCCORMICK, JOHN, born 1795, a shoemaker, session clerk of Iona, then a teacher in Catchean, died 1861. [M.332, 359, 450]

MCCORMICK, MURDOCH, born 1763, tenant of Uisken, died 23 October 1820. [Kilvickeon gravestone, Mull]

MCCOUSH, CHRISTY, born on Coll, wife of Donald, emigrated to Cape Breton in October 1840, with their infant child. [NSARM.RG5, series P]

MCCRUER, Reverend PATRICK, assistant preacher on Jura and Colonsay, a petition, 1802. [NRS.GD64.1.174]

MCCRUMMAN, DONALD, born 1819, Ann born 1820, Marion born 1843, Margaret born 1846, Donald born 1847, and Christy born 1851, from St Kilda, emigrated via Liverpool aboard the Priscilla bound for Victoria, Australia, on 15 October 1852. [NRS.HD4/5]

MCCUAIG, ALEXANDER, in Upper Killeyan, Islay, an illicit whisky distiller who was jailed in Inveraray in 1850. [NRS.CE81.6.2]

MCCUAIG, DUNCAN, born 1844, from Islay, emigrated via Glasgow aboard the Damascus bound for Toronto on 28 June 1862. [JRK]

MCCUAIG, ..., a widow, born 1804, Rachel born 1841, Duncan born 1843, Finlay born 1845, John born 1850, Janet born 1852, Catherine born 1854, and John born 1855, from Islay, emigrated via Glasgow aboard the Damascus bound for Toronto on 28 June 1862. [JRK]

MCCUAN, ANGUS, born 1803, Sarah born 1812, Donald born 1833, John born 1835, Christy born 1837, Murdoch born 1839, Ann born 1843, and Flora born 1845, from Herlista, [Herbusta?], Skye, emigrated via Liverpool aboard the Priscilla bound for Victoria, Australia, on 15 October 1852. [NRS.HD4/5]

MCDERMIT, NEIL, with Margaret, from Skye aboard the Malay bound for Sydney, Nova Scotia, in 1830. [NSARM.RG1.67/19]

MCDIARMID, ALEXANDER, born 1825, from North Uist, emigrated via Greenock aboard the Waterhen of London bound for Quebec in 1849. [NRS.GD221.4435]

MCDIARMID, DIARMID, born 1799 on Islay, died in North Carolina on 30 January 1874. [Longstreet Presbyterian gravestone, Fort Bragg, Hoke County, N.C.]

MCDIARMID, DONALD, from Borve, [Na Buirgh], Skye, died 1833 in South Carolina. [Inverness Courier, 5.2.1834] [NRS.RS38.GR2241/239]

MCDIARMID, DONALD, born 1818, Malcolm born 1839, from Stein Skeabost, [Steinn Sgeubost], Skye, emigrated via Plymouth to Van Diemen's Land, Australia, aboard the Louisa on 24 September 1852. [NRS.HD4/5]

MCDIARMID, HUGH, a crofter in Craigfade, Islay, was accused of deforcement in 1819. [NRS.AD14.19.27]

MCDONALD, A. L., a writer in Tobermory, Mull, a letter 1843. [NRS.GD174.277]

MACDONALD, Reverend ALEXANDER, the priest on Uist, a letter dated 24 January 1800. [NRA.NRAS.2177, bundle 106]

MCDONALD, ALEXANDER, emigrated from Skye to North Carolina in 1800, settled in Moore County, N.C. [NCSA]

MCDONALD, Colonel ALEXANDER, of Boisdale, South Uist, and his wife Marion, a letter dated 1 June 1802. [NRS.NRAS.2177.1512]

MCDONALD, ALEXANDER, born 1803, a crofter in Ulva later in Tobermory, Mull, with his wife Flora, and children Coll born 1835, Lachlan born 1837, Donald born 1839, Mary, born 1844, Marion born 1848, and Julian born 1852, evicted, emigrated

PEOPLE OF THE HEBRIDES, 1800-1850

aboard the Panama bound for Van Diemen's Land, Australia, in 1853. [NRS.HD4/5]

MCDONALD, ALEXANDER, tenant in Lephain, died 15 December 1808, father of Dugald died 2 June 1803. [Tobermory gravestone]

MCDONALD, ALEXANDER, of Harris, rental of Harris, 1818. [NRS.GD1.421.125]

MACDONALD, ALEXANDER, tenant of Ardellum, Ulva, in 1824. [NRS.GD174.1140.9]

MCDONALD, ALEXANDER, son of John McDonald, tacksman of Scalpaig, and his wife Barbara Tolmie, emigrated to Charleston, South Carolina, in December1845, later settled in Georgia. [NRS.GD403.70]

MCDONALD, ALEXANDER J., born 1824 on Uist, [Uibhist], died on Long Island, Cape Breton, on 30 May 1906. [St Andrew's RC cemetery, Boisdale, Cape Breton.]

MCDONALD, ALEXANDER, born 1779, Flora born 1789, Donald born 1821, Margaret born 1823, Flora born 1825, John born 1826, Marion born 1827, Ann born 1829, William born 1827, from North Uist, emigrated via Greenock aboard the Waterhen of London bound for Quebec in 1849. [NRS.GD221.4435]

MCDONALD, ALEXANDER, born 1794, Margaret born 1800, Effy born 1825, Donald born 1828, Catherine born 1831, Murdoch 1834, Mary born 1836, and Ann born 1844, from Sheader, Uig, [Siader, An Uig], Skye, emigrated via Liverpool aboard the Priscilla bound for Victoria, Australia, on 15 October 1852. [NRS.HD4/5]

MCDONALD, ALEXANDER, born 1799, Catherine born 1812, Allan born 1823, Donald born 1826, Roderick born 1830, Archibald born 1832, John born 1835, Christy born 1844, and

Marion born 1848, from North Uist, emigrated via Greenock aboard the Waterhen of London bound for Quebec in 1849. [NRS.GD221.4435]

MCDONALD, ALEXANDER, born 1810, Mary born 1811, Flora born 1832, Norman born 1839, Mary born 1841, Christy born 1845, and Duncan born 1848, from Rhea, Uig, emigrated via Liverpool aboard the Priscilla bound for Victoria, Australia, on 15 October 1852. [NRS.HD4/5]

MCDONALD, ALEXANDER, born 1830, from North Uist, emigrated via Greenock aboard the Waterhen of London bound for Quebec in 1849. [NRS.GD221.4435]

MCDONALD, ALEXANDER, born 1804, Isobel born 1803, James born 1829, Ian born 1831, Angus born 1833, Alexander born 1838, from North Uist, emigrated via Greenock aboard the Waterhen of London bound for Quebec in 1849. [NRS.GD221.4435]

MCDONALD, ALEXANDER, and family, from Fairfield, Skye, emigrated to Australia aboard the Arabian in 1854. [NRS.GD221.4437.1]

MCDONALD, ALEXANDER, and his wife, from Valtos, Skye, emigrated to Australia aboard the Arabian in 1854. [NRS.GD221.4437.1]

MCDONALD, ALEXANDER, son of John McDonald, the tacksman of Scalpaig, and his wife Barbara Tolmie, emigrated to Charleston, South Carolina, in 1845, died in Enterprise, Georgia, in 1859. [NRS.GD403.70]

MACDONALD, ALEXANDER, born 1817, Christina born 1817, Christina born 1842, Marion born 1845, Catherine born 1848, Mary born 1849, and Maybel born 1854, emigrated from Harris aboard the Clansman bound for Australia on 13 July 1857. [NRS.GD371.241.1]

MCDONALD, ALLAN, with family, from Cleadale, Eigg, emigrated via Arisaig aboard The British Queen of Greenock to Quebec in 1790. [NAC.RG4A1.48.15874-5]

MCDONALD, ALLAN, born 1770 in South Uist, with his wife Mary McLean, emigrated to Canada in 1822, settled in Whucocomagh, Cape Breton. [SG.33.2.199]

MACDONALD, ALLAN, from South Uist, emigrated aboard the Emperor Alexander of Aberdeen, master Alexander Watt, from Tobermory, Mull, to Sydney, Cape Breton, in July 1823, landed on 16 September 1823. [Inverness Journal, 30 January 1824]

MCDONALD, ANDREW, born 1751, with Janet McDonald born 1770, and Hugh born 1791, from Tobermory, Mull, aboard the brig Isle of Skye bound for Prince Edward Island in 1806. [PAPEI.2702]

MCDONALD, ANGUS, from the Isle of Lewis, a soldier in the American War of Independence, died in Glenelg Northumberland County, New Brunswick, on 11 January 1842. [New Brunswick Courier, 22.1.1842.]

MCDONALD, ANGUS, born 1767, his wife Mary McLugash born 1772, Donald born 1794 a labourer, Jean born 1796, Anne born 1798, Archibald born 1796, and Alexander born 1804, from Balinhard, Kilnichen, [Cill Fhionnchain], Mull, emigrated to Hudson Bay in 1812. [NAC.SP[C1], 294, 558-561]

MCDONALD, ANGUS, born 1801 on Uist, [Uibhist], died 24 May 1866, his wife Mary Ross, born 1805 on Uist, died 11 December 1865, residents at Leitches Creek, Cape Breton. [St Andrew's RC cemetery, Boisdale, Cape Breton.]

MCDONALD, ANGUS, [fear Oainish mac Dhomhnull ic Sheumas], with his wife, the daughter of Reverend George Munro, and their family, were evicted from Oainish, South Uist, and sent to America in the 1840s. [SCA.DA9.43]

MCDONALD, ANGUS, Nancy McLaughlin, Allan McDonald born 1786, John McDonald born 1788, Archibald McDonald, Neil McDonald, Donald McDonald, Hector McDonald, from Oransay, emigrated to La Chine, Quebec, on board the Oughton in 1804. [PACAN. McDonell pp.105/8]

MCDONALD, ANGUS, born on North Uist in 1786, settled in Cape Breton in 1828, died 16 December 1857. [McCuish Cemetery, Richmond County, Nova Scotia]

MCDONALD, ANGUS, born 1746, Ann born 1756, Catherine born 1782, Donald born 1786, Christine born 1784, from Tobermory, Mull, aboard the brig Humphreys bound for Prince Edward Island in 1806. [PAPEI.2702]

MCDONALD, ANGUS, of Milton, South Uist, died 1806, edict of executry in 1808. [NRS.CC12.7.39.9]

MCDONALD, ANGUS, son of John McDonald at Stonybridge, South Uist, accused of assault in 1843. [NRS.AD14.43.21]

MCDONALD, ANGUS, born 1815, from North Uist, emigrated via Greenock aboard the Waterhen of London bound for Quebec in 1849. [NRS.GD221.4435]

MACDONALD, ANGUS, from North Uist, emigrated aboard the Emperor Alexander of Aberdeen, master Alexander Watt, from Tobermory, Mull, to Sydney, Cape Breton, in July 1823, landed on 16 September 1823. [Inverness Journal, 30 January 1824]

MCDONALD, ANGUS, born 1809, and Ann born 1824, from Bonessan, [Bun Easain], Mull, emigrated via Liverpool aboard the Marmion bound for Moreton Bay, Australia, on 28 August 1852. [NRS.HD4/5]

MCDONALD, ANGUS, with his wife, son, and daughter from Valtos, Skye, applied to emigrate to Australia in 1854. [NRS.GD221.4437.1]

MCDONALD, ANN, daughter of the late Hugh McDonald tacksman of Kilfedder, [Cill Pheadair], a lease of the farm of Kildonan, [Cill Donnain], on Eigg for nineteen years from 25 March 1819. [NRS.GD201.2.67]

MCDONALD, ANTONY, born 1770, priest of the Small Isles from 1782 until his death on Eigg on 6 January 1843. [IR.18.162]

MACDONALD, ARCHIBALD, tenant of Ferinardry, Ulva, in 1824. [NRS.GD174.1140.9]

MACDONALD, ARCHIBALD, a wright and tenant of Ardellum, Ulva, in 1824. [NRS.GD174.1140.9]

MACDONALD, ARCHIBALD, tenant of Ardellum, Ulva, in 1824. [NRS.GD174.1140.9]

MCDONALD, CATHERINE, born 1801, Neil born 1830, and Ann born 1837, from St Kilda, emigrated via Liverpool aboard the Priscilla bound for Victoria, Australia, on 15 October 1852. [NRS.HD4/5]

MCDONALD, CATHERINE, born 1837, emigrated from Harris on board the Clansman bound for Australia on 13 July 1857. [NRS.GD371.241.1]

MACDONALD, CHARLES, tenant farmer of Gillin, [Na Gilean], and Dalville, Skye, a contract, 1821. [NRS.NRAS.3273/4289]

MACDONALD, CHARLES, born 3 January 1808 on Tiree, settled in Nova Scotia, died 12 January 1856. [Little Narrows cemetery, Victoria County, Nova Scotia]

MACDONALD, CHRISTIAN, from South Uist, emigrated aboard the Emperor Alexander of Aberdeen, master Alexander Watt, from Tobermory, Mull, to Sydney, Cape Breton, in July 1823., landed on 16 September 1823. [Inverness Journal, 30 January 1824]

MCDONALD, CHRISTIAN, born 1776, a forger in Portree, Skye, in 1836. [NRS.AD14.36.40]

MCDONALD, CHRISTIAN, born 1821, from North Uist, emigrated via Greenock aboard the Waterhen of London bound for Quebec in 1849. [NRS.GD221.4435]

MCDONALD, CHRISTY, born 1806, Alexander born 1831, Mary born 1836, Archibald born 1841, and Keith born 1845, from Ferrindonald, [Fearann Domhnaill], Skye, emigrated via Liverpool aboard the Priscilla bound for Victoria, Australia, on 15 October 1852. [NRS.HD4/5]

MCDONALD, COLL, born 1833, son of Neil MacDonald and his wife Mary MacDougall in Siaba, Ross of Mull, a lobster fisher. [M.302/450]

MCDONALD, DAVID, in Dunvegan, Skye, letters, 1848. [NRS.HD10.22]

MCDONALD, DONALD, born 1782, from Tobermory, Mull, aboard the brig Humphreys bound for Prince Edward Island in 1806. [PAPEI.2702]

MCDONALD, DONALD, a tenant in Cleadale, [Cleadail], Eigg, with family, emigrated via Arisaig aboard The British Queen of Greenock to Quebec in 1790. [NAC.RG4A1.48.15874-5]

MCDONALD, DONALD, with his family of five, from Armadale, Sleat, emigrated via Drimindarroch, [Druim an Daraich], on board the Jane bound for Prince Edward Island in July 1790. [SCA]

MCDONALD, DONALD, born 1772, a tailor, Flora born 1778, John born 1798, Duncan born 1799, and Hugh born 1800, from Tiree, emigrated to La Chine, Quebec, on board the Oughton in 1804. [PACAN. McDonell pp.105/8]

MCDONALD, DONALD, a clerk in Lyndale, [Lianadail], Skye, 1812. [NRS.AD14.12.36]

MACDONALD, DONALD, tenant of Ferinardry, Ulva, in 1824. [NRS.GD174.1140.9]

MACDONALD, DONALD, tenant of Ballygartan, Ulva, in 1824. [NRS.GD174.1140.9]

MACDONALD, DONALD, tenant of Berniss, [Bearnas], Ulva, in 1824. [NRS.GD174.1140.9]

MCDONALD, DONALD, from North Uist, emigrated to Canada in 1827, died on 12 June 1851. [Stewartdale gravestone, Whycocomagh, Nova Scotia]

MCDONALD, DONALD, son of John McDonald, tacksman of Scalpaig, and his wife Barbara Tolmie, emigrated via Liverpool to New York in 1840. [NRS.GD403.70]

MCDONALD, DONALD, born 1807, Marion born 1809, Mary born 1829, Archibald born 1833, Christy born 1835, Flora born 1838, Helen born 1840, John born 1842, Donald born 1844, William born 1846, from Portree, Skye, emigrated via Liverpool aboard the Araminta bound for Geelong, Australia, on 20 June 1852. [NRS.HD4/5]

MCDONALD, DONALD, born 1812, Flora born 1819, Mary born 1835, Catherine born 1837, Myles born 1843, Angus born 1848, and Sarah born 1851, from Faull, emigrated via Liverpool aboard the Araminta bound for Geelong, Australia, on 20 June 1852. [NRS.HD4/5]

MCDONALD, DONALD, son of the late Roderick McDonald in Strond, Harris, a petition, 1817. [NRS.CC12.6.8.4]

MCDONALD, DONALD, born 1819, his wife born 1826, Charles born 1849, Ewen born 1851, from Sconser, Skye, emigrated via Liverpool aboard the Borneuf bound for Geelong, Australia, on 26 May 1852. [NRS.HD4/5]

MCDONALD, DONALD, with Bell and son Duncan and stepsons Colin, Charles, and Lachlan Campbell, from Skye aboard the

Malay bound for Sydney, Nova Scotia, in 1830. [NSARM.RG1.67/19]

MCDONALD, DONALD, born in 1797 on North Uist, emigrated to Canada in 1827, died 12 June 1851. [Stewartdale gravestone, Whycocomagh, Nova Scotia]

MCDONALD, DONALD, born 1799, Catherine born1799, Roderick born1825, and Donald born 1829, from North Uist, emigrated via Greenock aboard the Waterhen of London bound for Quebec in 1849. [NRS.GD221.4435]

MCDONALD, DONALD, born 1831, from North Uist, emigrated via Greenock aboard the Waterhen of London bound for Quebec in 1849. [NRS.GD221.4435]

MACDONALD, DONALD, from South Uist, emigrated aboard the Emperor Alexander of Aberdeen, master Alexander Watt, from Tobermory, Mull, to Sydney, Cape Breton, in July 1823., landed on 16 September 1823. [Inverness Journal, 30 January 1824]

MCDONALD, DONALD, of Tarnera, son of James McDonald of Skeabost [Sgeubost], Skye, a charter, 1819. [NRS.GD23.4.258]

MCDONALD, DONALD, born 1807, with wife Marion born 1810, and children Mary born 1829, Archibald born 1833, Christy born 1835, Flora born 1838, Helen born 1840, John born 1842, Donald born 1844, and William born 1846, from Portree, Skye, emigrated aboard the Araminta to Geelong, Australia, in 1852. [NRS.HD.4/5]

MCDONALD, DONALD, of Skeabost, [Sgeubost], Skye, a decreet, 1821. [NRS.CS44.189.76]; a letter, 1828, [NRS.GD23.6.630]; a memorandum, 1822, [NRS.GD90.2.252]

MCDONALD, DONALD, possibly from Skye, a grocer in Thomasville, Florida, in 1841. [NRS.NRAS.0427]

MCDONALD, DONALD, born 1827, from North Uist, emigrated via Greenock aboard the <u>Waterhen of London</u> bound for Quebec in 1849. [NRS.GD221.4435]

MCDONALD, DONALD, born 1819, his wife born 1826, Charles born 1849, and Ewen born 1851, from Sconser, Skye, emigrated via Liverpool aboard the <u>Borneuf</u> bound for Geelong, Australia, on 26 May 1852. [NRS.HD4/5]

MCDONALD, DONALD, with his wife, four sons and four daughters, from Scullamus, Skye, emigrated on board the <u>Edward Johnston</u> bound for Australia in 1854. [NRS.GD221.4437.1]

MCDONALD, DOUGAL, a joint-tenant of Auchenadeunie, Lismore, [Liosmor], a letter to Sir Duncan Campbell of Barcaldine, his landlord, re inability to pay rent, 1824. [NRS.GD170.2349]

MACDONALD, DUGALD, a tenant of Ormag, Ulva, in 1824. [NRS.GD174.1087.1]

MACDONALD, DUGALD, his wife, and family in Drimore, Carry, South Uist, were evicted in the 1840s and sent to America. [SCA.DA9.43]

MCDONALD, DUNCAN, with Christy, and children Flora and Donald, from Skye aboard the <u>Malay</u> bound for Sydney, Nova Scotia, in 1830. [NSARM.RG1.67/19]

MCDONALD, DUNCAN, born 1821, died 9 November 1843. [Kilpatrick Duart gravestone, Torosay]

MCDONALD, DUNCAN, with Anne, from Skye aboard the <u>Malay</u> bound for Sydney, Nova Scotia, in 1830. [NSARM.RG1.67/19]

MCDONALD, or LAMOND, FLORA, wife of Donald McDonald in Ullinish, Bracadale, Skye, accused of bigamy with John McKinnon in Ballemore, Durinish, [Diuranais], Skye, in 1837. [NRS.AD14.37.343]

PEOPLE OF THE HEBRIDES, 1800-1850

MCDONALD, HARRY, a writer in Portree, Skye, in 1832.
[NRS.CS96.172]

MACDONALD, HECTOR, tenant of Cragaig, Ulva, in 1824.
[NRS.GD174.1140.9]

MCDONALD, HUGH, born 1770 on Sleat, died in Moore County,
North Carolina on 11 April 1860. [NCPresbyterian.28.4.1860]

MCDONALD, HUGH, born 1774, Janet McDonald born 1783,
Betty born 1804, and Angus born 1806, aboard the brig Isle of
Skye bound from Tobermory, Mull, for Prince Edward Island in
1806. [PAPEI.2702]

MCDONALD, HUGH, born 1783, from Tobermory, Mull, aboard
the brig Isle of Skye bound for Prince Edward Island in 1806.
[PAPEI.2702]

MCDONALD, HUGH, born 1833, in the West Indies, died 5
October 1852, husband of Lucy Clark, born 1824, died 9
September 1893. [Kilpatrick Duart gravestone, Torosay]

MACDONALD, HUGH, a shepherd in Fishnish, Mull, in 1831.
[M.312]

MCDONALD, HUGH, with his aunt and a brother, from Uig,
Skye, applied to emigrate to Australia in 1854.
[NRS.GD221.4437.1]

MCDONALD, ISABELLA, from Cleadale, Eigg, emigrated via
Arisaig aboard The British Queen of Greenock to Quebec in
1790. [NAC.RG4A1.48.15874-5]

MACDONALD, HUGH, tenant of Ardellum, Ulva, in 1824.
[NRS.GD174.1140.9]

MCDONALD, HUGH, born 1797, died on Lismore on 10
November 1847, husband of Ann McCaig, born 1798, died 12
April 1874. [Lismore gravestone]

MCDONALD, ISABELLA, in Eriskay, letter re a liquor licence, 1807. [NRS.GD23.6.435]

MCDONALD, JAMES THOMAS, in Balranald, Dunvegan, Skye, victim of a crime in 1837. [NRS.AD14.37.35]

MCDONALD, JANET, born 1823, from North Uist, emigrated via Greenock aboard the Waterhen of London bound for Quebec in 1849. [NRS.GD221.4435]

MACDONALD, JOHN, a tenant of Lord MacDonald in Balmaqueen, Skye, was bound for America around 1802. [NRS.GD221.4433.1]

MCDONALD, JOHN, emigrated from Skye to Cumberland County, North Carolina, in 1802. [NCSA.2.65]

MCDONALD, JOHN, born 1769, tenant in Dervaig, died 7 October 1834. [Kilmore Dervaig gravestone, Mull]

MACDONALD, JOHN, a tenant of Lord MacDonald in Peigown and Osmigarry, Skye, was bound for America around 1802. [NRS.GD221.4433.1]

MCDONALD, JOHN, of Borrodale, factor of the Clanranald estates on Canna, Eigg, Moidart and Arisaig, 1819-1821. [NRS.GD210.5.311]

MCDONALD, JOHN, son of Alexander McDonald of Drimindarach, a surgeon on South Uist, emigrated to America in 1824. [CD]

MCDONALD, JOHN, born 1803, Mary born1805, Catherine born1828, Christy born 1830, Duncan born 1833, Mary born 1834, Jonathan born 1836, John Born 1838, Ann born 1840, and Ann born 1842, from North Uist, emigrated via Greenock aboard the Waterhen of London bound for Quebec in 1849. [NRS.GD221.4435]

MCDONALD, JOHN, tenant farmer of Skeirinsh, parish of Snizort, Skye, contract, 1825. [NRS.NRAS.3273/4289]

MACDONALD, JOHN, tenant of Eolasary, Ulva, in 1824. [NRS.GD174.1140.9]

MACDONALD, JOHN, tenant of Glaknagallon, Ulva, in 1824. [NRS.GD174.1140.9]

MACDONALD, JOHN, tenant of Culinish, Ulva, in 1824. [NRS.GD174.1140.9]

MACDONALD, JOHN, tenant of Ferinardry, Ulva, in 1824. [NRS.GD174.1140.9]

MCDONALD, JOHN, born 1812, his wife born 1813. Rachel born 1833, Ewen born 1835, Mary born 1837, Christian born 1841, Donald born 1843, Alexander born 1846, Catherine born 1848, and Flora born 1850, from Point of Sleat, Sleat, emigrated via Liverpool aboard the Mangerton bound for Melbourne, Australia, on 26 January 1852. [NRS.HD.4/5]

MCDONALD, JOHN, born 1816, died at Port Ramsay on 17 April 1896, husband of Janet McIntyre, born 1818, died 9 April 1891. [Lismore gravestone]

MCDONALD, JOHN, born 1823, from North Uist, emigrated via Greenock aboard the Waterhen of London bound for Quebec in 1849. [NRS.GD221.4435]

MCDONALD, JOHN, born 1825, Catherine born 1827, Marion born 1855, and Rory born 1856, emigrated from Harris aboard the Clansman bound for Australia on 13 July 1857. [NRS.GD371.241.1]

MCDONALD, JOHN, born 1832, Mary born 1837, and Norman born 1856, emigrated from Harris aboard the Clansman bound for Australia on 13 July 1857. [NRS.GD371.241.1]

MCDONALD, JOHN, born 1813, Mary born 1815, Angus born 1833, Norman born 1842, Ann born 1839 and Alexander born 1841, emigrated from Harris aboard the Clansman bound for Australia on 13 July 1857. [NRS.GD371.241.1]

MCDONALD, JOHN, jr., born 1835, wife Margaret born 1837, emigrated from Harris aboard the Clansman bound for Australia on 13 July 1857. [NRS.GD371.241.1]

MCDONALD, Captain KENNETH, of Skeabost, Skye, inventory, 1814. [NRS.CC12.5.4.2]

MCDONALD, KENNETH, in Skeabost, Skye, letters, 1848. [NRS.HD10.23]

MCDONALD, LAUCHLIN, born 1795, from Tobermory, Mull, aboard the brig Humphreys bound for Prince Edward Island in 1806. [PAPEI.2702]

MACDONALD, LACHLAN, tenant of Upper Kilvickewan, Ulva, in 1824. [NRS.GD174.1140.9]

MACDONALD, LACHLAN, tenant of the Ulva Inn, in 1824. [NRS.GD174.1140.9]

MCDONALD, MAGGIE, from Erlish, Skye, a servant maid in Portree, Skye, applied to emigrate to Australia in 1854. [NRS.GD221.4437.1]

MCDONALD, MALCOLM, on the south side of Lochboisdale, South Uist, letter re a liquor licence, 1807. [NRS.GD23.6.435]

MCDONALD, MALCOLM, minister of Gigha, 1814. [NRS.CS271.62975]

MACDONALD, MALCOLM, born 1820 on Harris, [Na Hearadh], died in Nova Scotia in 1892. [Pinehill gravestone, NS]

MACDONALD, MALCOLM, from North Uist, emigrated aboard the Emperor Alexander of Aberdeen, master Alexander Watt, from Tobermory, Mull, to Sydney, Cape Breton, in July 1823, landed on 16 September 1823. [Inverness Journal, 30 January 1824]

MACDONALD, MALCOLM, tenant of Culinish, Ulva, in 1824. [NRS.GD174.1140.9]

MCDONALD, MARGARET, born 1809, daughter of John McDonald tenant in Tigharry, North Uist, 1832. [NRS.JC26.1832.123]

MCDONALD, MARGARET, born 1822, Catherine born 1837, and Lachlan born 1834, from Uig, emigrated via Liverpool aboard the Priscilla bound for Victoria, Australia, on 15 October 1852. [NRS.HD4/5]

MCDONALD, MARY, born 1756, emigrated to La Chine, Quebec, on board the Oughton in 1804. [PACAN. McDonell pp.105/8]

MCDONALD, MARY, born 1786, from Tobermory, Mull, aboard the brig Isle of Skye bound for Prince Edward Island in 1806. [PAPEI.2702]

MCDONALD, MARY, born 1771, with Margaret Cameron born 1796, and Duncan Cameron born 1799, from Tobermory, Mull, aboard the brig Isle of Skye bound for Prince Edward Island in 1806. [PAPEI.2702]

MCDONALD, NEIL, born 1803, son of Murdoch McDonald tenant in Scarristermore, Harris, accused of theft in 1822. [NRS.AD14.22.244]

MACDONALD, NIEL, tenant of Ballygartan, Ulva, in 1824. [NRS.GD174.1140.9]

MACDONALD, NIEL, tenant of Berniss, Ulva, in 1824. [NRS.GD174.1140.9]

MACDONALD, NORMAN, a smith at the Sound of Ulva, 1824. [NRS.GD174.1140.9]

MCDONALD, PETER, a tenant of Cragaig, Ulva, in 1824. [NRS.GD174.1087.1]

MCDONALD, R., a landowner in Mull and Ulva in 1819. [NRS.RH9.3.90]

MACDONALD, RANALD, of Ulva, a letter, 1803. [NRS.248.656.3]

MCDONALD, RANALD, of Staffa, versus Elizabeth Steuart, daughter of Sir Henry Steuart of Allanton, process of divorce, 1830, [NRS.CC8.6.2192; GD16.41.1088; GD16.32.19]

MACDONALD, RANALD, born 1715 in Vallay, [Bhalaigh], North Uist, settled in Whycocomagh, Cape Breton, in 1828. [SG.33.2.199]

MACDONALD, RODERICK, born 1763, from Garrfluich, South Uist, ordained in 1791, priest in South Uist and Benbecula, died there on 29 September 1828. [IR.18.163]

MCDONALD, RODERICK, born 12 April 1804 in Snizort, Skye, son of Alexander McDonald and his wife Christian McLeod, a Brevet Captain of the 69th Bengal Native Infantry, died on 3 March 1837 in Edinburgh. [BA.3.127]

MCDONALD, RODERICK, born 1829, from North Uist, emigrated via Greenock aboard the Waterhen of London bound for Quebec in 1849. [NRS.GD221.4435]

MCDONALD, RODERICK, born 1817, Euphemia born 1823, John born 1848, from North Uist, emigrated via Greenock aboard the Waterhen of London bound for Quebec in 1849. [NRS.GD221.4435]

MCDONALD, RODERICK, born 1805, Marion born 1804, Neil born 1837, and Christy born 1834, from St Kilda, emigrated via Liverpool aboard the Priscilla bound for Victoria, Australia, on 15 October 1852. [NRS.HD4/5]

MCDONALD, RONALD, born 1771, Mary McDonald born 1772, Margaret born 1801, and Mary born 1804, from Tobermory, Mull, aboard the brig Isle of Skye bound for Prince Edward Island in 1806. [PAPEI.2702]

MCDONALD, RONALD, born 1821, from North Uist, emigrated via Greenock aboard the Waterhen of London bound for Quebec in 1849. [NRS.GD221.4435]

MCDONALD, RONALD, born 1808, Marion born 1810, with Ann born 1835, Kitty born 1836, Duncan born 1838, Mary born 1841, Neil born 1845, and Peggy born 1845, from North Uist, [Uibhist a Tuath], emigrated via Greenock aboard the Cashmere of Glasgow bound for Quebec in 1849. [NRS.GD221.4011.53]

MCDONALD, WILLIAM, son of John McDonald, tacksman of Scalpaig, and his wife Barbara Tolmie, emigrated to Mobile in 1838, died in Texas in 1850. [NRS.GD403.70]

MCDONALD of Skeabost, Skye, ten letters, 1793-1811. [NRS.GD128.65.18]

MCDONALD and ELDER, merchants on Oronsay, 1814. [NRS.CS228.B14. 86]

MACDOUGALL, ALEXANDER, innkeeper at Scallacastle, Mull, was evicted in 1800. [M.284]

MCDOUGALL, ALEXANDER, a whisky distiller in Lagavullin in 1801. [NRS.JP36.5.46]

MCDOUGALL, DUGALD, a merchant in Tarbert, Gigha, 18.. [NRS.CS2.9.68]

MCDOUGALL, HECTOR, in Cliad, Coll,1832. [NRS.AD14.32.158]

MCDUGALL, HECTOR, born 1809, Ann born 1809, Catherine born 1847, and John born 1851, from Kilninian, [Cill Naoi Nighean], Mull, emigrated via Liverpool aboard the Marmion bound for Moreton Bay, Australia, on 28 August 1852. [NRS.HD4/5]

MCDOUGALL, HUGH, schoolmaster in Craighouse, [Taigh na Creige], Jura, 1818. [NRS.GD64.1.112]

MCDOUGALL, HUGH, tenant in Roskernie, Islay, 1818. [NRS.GD64.1.112]

MACDOUGALL, MALCOLM, from Barra, emigrated aboard the Emperor Alexander of Aberdeen, master Alexander Watt, from Tobermory, Mull, to Sydney, Cape Breton, in July 1823, landed on 16 September 1823. [Inverness Journal, 30 January 1824]

MCDOUGAL, NEIL, born 1787, from North Uist, with Ann born 1795, William born 1819, Mary born 1831, John born 1833, Archibald born 1839, Margaret born 1841, and Mary born 1844, from North Uist, emigrated via Greenock aboard the Waterhen of London bound for Quebec in 1849. [NRS.GD221.4435]

MCDOUGAL, PEGGY, from Cleadale, Eigg, with family, emigrated via Arasaig aboard The British Queen of Greenock to Quebec in 1790. [NAC.RG4A1.48.15874-5]

MCDOUALL, ALLAN, born 1829, from North Uist, emigrated via Greenock aboard the Waterhen of London bound for Quebec in 1849. [NRS.GD221.4435]

MCDOUALL, WILLIAM, born 1827, from North Uist, emigrated via Greenock aboard the Waterhen of London bound for Quebec in 1849. [NRS.GD221.4435]

MCDOUGALL, JOHN, a whisky distiller in Ardbeg, Islay, in 1818.

MCDOUGALL, MALCOLM, born 1791, shoemaker at Penmore, died 14 January 1868, husband of Janet McLean, born 1806, died 7 July 1873. [Calgary, [Calgarraidh], gravestone, Mull]

MCDUFFIE, JOHN, tenant in Barr, Islay, 1818. [NRS.GD64.1.112]

MCDUFFIE, JOHN, a whisky distiller at Kintour, Islay, in 1818.

MCDUGALD, ARCHIBALD, tenant of Soriby, Ulva, in 1824. [NRS.GD174.1140.9]

MCDUGALD, JOHN, tenant of Glaknagallon, Ulva, in 1824. [NRS.GD174.1140.9]

MCDUGALD, Mrs MARGARET, born on Islay, relict of Hugh McDugald, died 1862 in Bladen County, North Carolina. [NC Presbyterian, 12.7.1862]

MCDUSSIE, ARCHIBALD, from Jamaica, died on Islay in 1806. [AJ.3052]

MCEACHERN, ANGUS, born 1734, from Tobermory, Mull, aboard the brig Isle of Skye bound for Prince Edward Island in 1806. [PAPEI.2702]

MCEACHARN, ANN, born 1756, Charles born 1789, from Tobermory, Mull, aboard the brig Humphreys bound for Prince Edward Island in 1806. [PAPEI.2702]

MCEACHERN, ARCHIBALD, born 1776, Sarah born 1776, Jane born 1800, Lauchlin born 1803, Margaret born 1806, from Tobermory, Mull, aboard the brig Humphreys bound for Prince Edward Island in 1806. [PAPEI.2702]

MCEACHERN, DONALD, a whisky distiller at Ballachlaven, Islay, in 1801. [NRS.JP36.5.46]

MCEACHERN, DONALD, born 1766, Mary McGilvray born 1771, Angus born 1793, Catherine born 1795, Archibald born 1803, and John born 1804, aboard the brig Isle of Skye bound from Tobermory, Mull, for Prince Edward Island in 1806. [PAPEI.2702]

MCEACHERN, DONALD, born 1746, Sarah born 1754, Donald born 1782, Mary born 1787, Dugald born 1788, Janet born 1794, Hector born 1797, from Tobermory, Mull, aboard the brig Humphreys bound for Prince Edward Island in 1806. [PAPEI.2702]

MCEACHERN, DONALD, a whisky distiller at Bridgend, Islay, in 1818; a merchant and distiller at Bridgend, Islay, 1821-1824. [NRS.CS96.3694]

MCEACHERN, DONALD, eldest son of the late Neil McEachern, tenant of the pendicle of Inishroll, Mull, in 1838. [NRS.C50.5.1838.38]

MCEACHERN, FARQUHAR, in Leogin, Kilmany, Islay, was accused of plundering a ship, in 1812. [NRS.AD14.92]

MCEACHERN, HECTOR, servant of McNeill of Colonsay, was accused of theft in 1821. [NRS.AD14.21.116]

MCEACHERN, HUGH, tenant in Kinloch, husband of Catherine Shaw, born 1772, died 12 March 1827, parents of Duncan, born 1811, died 1829. [Killunaig gravestone, Mull]

MCEACHERN, JOHN, born 1784, Sarah born 1776, Jane born 1800, Margaret born 1806, from Tobermory, Mull, aboard the brig Humphreys bound for Prince Edward Island in 1806. [PAPEI.2702]

MCEACHERN, MALCOLM, with Mary his wife, from Skibbo, Kilchoman, Islay, emigrated aboard the Prince of Wales bound for the Red River Settlement in 1813. [PAC.M155,165-168]

MCEACHARN, MARY, born 1748, aboard the brig Isle of Skye bound from Tobermory, Mull, for Prince Edward Island in 1806. [PAPEI.2702]

MCEACHARN, MARY, born 1769, aboard the brig Isle of Skye bound from Tobermory, Mull, for Prince Edward Island in 1806. [PAPEI.702]

MCEACHERN, MARY, a widow, born 1788, Dugald born 1811, Hugh born 1812, Angus born 1815, John born 1817, Ronald born 1823, Rory born 1825, James born 1827, Peggy born 1821, and Mary born 1830, emigrated from Tobermory, Mull, on board the Catherine of Belfast on 13 July 1843 bound for Canada, were transferred to the John and Robert from Belfast on1 September 1843 bound for the Gut of Canso, Cape Breton.[PANS.CS88.M112]

MCEACHERN, NEIL, a whisky distiller at Bridgend, Islay, in 1801. [NRS.JP36.5.46]

MCEACHERN, NEIL, a whisky distiller in Daill, Islay, in 1818.

MCEACHERN, PETER, of Daill, a merchant in Islay, by 1802.

MCEACHRON, JOHN, born 1778, a labourer from Mull, wife Margaret born 1773, children Hugh born 1798, Alexander born 1801, Janet born 1803, also step-daughter Catherine Lamont born 1794, emigrated from Oban aboard the Claredon of Hull bound for Charlottetown, Prince Edward Island, in 1808. [TNA.CO226.23]

MCEWAN, DONALD, born 1802, tenant in Upper Killean, parish of Oa, Islay, his wife born 1806, Andrew born 1842, Neil born 1848, Duncan born 1850, Archibald born 1855, and Barbara born 1857, emigrated via Glasgow on board the Damascus bound for Toronto, Canada, on 28 June 1862. [JRK]

MCFADYEN, ALLEN, born on Tiree in 1813, died 14 July 1878, and his wife Jane, born on Tiree in 1809, died 17 February 1899. [Little Narrows cemetery, Victoria County, Nova Scotia]

MCFADYEN, ARCHIBALD, born 1754 on Islay, died in North Carolina in 1830. [Longstreet gravestone, Fort Bragg, Hoke County, N.C.]

MCFADYEN, ARCHIBALD, born on Tiree in 1782, died 10 January 1869, and his wife Mary, born on Tiree in 1789, died 10 July 1869. [Little Narrows cemetery, Victoria County, Nova Scotia]

MCFADYEN, DONALD, born 1774 on Coll, married Flora McLean in 1797, with children Hector, Anne, Donald, John, and Angus, emigrated via Greenock on board the St Lawrence bound for Ships Harbour, Cape Breton, on 12 July 1828. [SG.3.83]

MCFADYEN, JOHN, born 1801 on Skye, emigrated from Scotland to Charleston, South Carolina, in 1819, settled in Richmond County, NC, died on 23 June 1863. [NC Presbyterian, 1.8.1863]; born in Scotland, a farmer in Richmond County, aged 53, wife Barbara born 1808 in N.C., son Archibald born 1832 in N.C. [1850 Census]

MCFADYEN, LACHLAN, born 1824, Christy born 1825, Flora born 1851, and Ann an infant, from Arynagour, [Airigh nan Gobhar], Coll, emigrated via Liverpool aboard the Marmion bound for Moreton Bay, Australia, on 28 August 1852. [NRS.HD4/5]

MCFARLANE, ANDREW, tenant of Ferinardry, Ulva, in 1824. [NRS.GD174.1140.9]

MCFARLANE, DUGALD, born 1813, a crofter/fisherman in Tobermory, Mull, with wife Effy born 1818, and children Lachlan born 1839, Lachlan born 1841, Donald born 1841,

Mary born 1843, Ann born 1845, Neil born 1847, Kate born 1849, and Sally born 1852, emigrated aboard the Panama bound for Van Diemen's Land, Australia, in 1853. [NRS.HD4/5]

MCFARLANE, HUGH, born 1792, boat builder, died at Ardun on 4 February 1876, husband of Ann McIntyre who died 13 July 1854. [Kilpatrick gravestone, Mull]

MCFARLANE, JOHN, born 1804, Sally born 1807, Hugh born 1833, Alexander born 1835, John born 1838, Malcolm born 1840, Mary born 1844, and Flora born 1848, from Tobermory, Mull, emigrated via Liverpool on the Marmion bound for Moreton Bay, Australia, on 28 August 1852. [NRS.HD4/5]

MACFARLANE, MARY, a widow, born 1804, Dugald born 1824, Ronald born 1828, Archibald born 1831, Christian born 1833, Archibald born 1836, from Iona, emigrated via Liverpool aboard the Marmion bound for Moreton Bay, Australia, on 28 August 1852. [NRS.HD4/5]33,

MACFARLANE,......, a widow, a tenant of Ormaig, Ulva, in 1824. [NRS.GD174.1087.1]

MCFARQUHAR, JAMES, a gardener in Lyndale, [Lianadail], Skye, 1812. [NRS.AD14.12.36]

MCFEE, DONALD, born 1802, Mary born 1802, Neil born 1822, Hector born 1824, Catherine born 1826, Mary born 1828, Alexander born 1830, Angus born 1833, Margaret born 1838, and Flora born 1841, from Renitra, Ross of Mull, emigrated via Liverpool aboard the Marmion bound for Moreton Bay, Australia, on 28 August 1852. [NRS.HD4/5]

MCGEACHY, DONALD, a wool carder and waulk miller at Sorn near Bridgend, Islay, in 1851. [I.247]

MCGIBBON, NEIL, of Glasvar, a decreet of absolvitor, 1819. [NRS.CS36.26.11]

MCGIBBON, DONALD, in Lower Killeyan, Islay, an illicit whisky distiller who was jailed in Inveraray in 1850. [NRS.CE81.6.2]

MCGIBBON, NEIL, in Lower Killeyan, Islay, an illicit whisky distiller who was jailed in Inveraray in 1850. [NRS.CE81.6.2]

MCGIBBON, WALTER, the younger of Glasvar, a decreet of absolvitor, 1819. [NRS.CS36.26.11]

MCGILL, ROBERT, tenant of the pendicle of Ballebrenan, Mull, in 1838. [NRS.C50.5.1838.38]

MCGILLIVRAY, ALEXANDER, in Bowmore, Islay, accused of theft in 1821. [NRS.AD14.21.209]

MCGILVRAY, Mrs ANNE, born 1771 on Mull, emigrated to America in 1791, widow of Donald McGregor, died at Haymount, North Carolina, on 18 June 1862. [NCPresbyterian,28.6.1862]

MCGILVRA, ARCHIBALD, born 1761, tacksman of Carvolg, died in 1819. [Kilpatrick gravestone, Mull]

MCGILLIVRAY, ARCHIBALD, in Bowmore, Islay, accused of theft in 1821. [NRS.AD14.21.209]

MCGILVRAY, DONALD, born 20 April 1772 on Skye, emigrated to America on 5 January 1804, died in North Carolina on 28 December 1854, [Cross Creek gravestone, N.C.]

MCGILVARY, DONALD, born 20 September 1772 on Skye, settled in North Carolina by 1809, died in Fayetteville, N.C., ON 28 December 1854. [CS.253]

MCGILVRAY, DONALD, son of John McGilvray tenant at the west end of Iona, accused of forgery in 1824. [NRS.AD14.24.205]

MCGILLIVRAY, DONALD, with wife, and two sons, in Portree, Skye, applied to emigrate to Australia in 1854. [NRS.GD221.4437.1]

MCGILVRAY, JAMES, died 2 September 1828. [Kilvickeon gravestone, Mull]

MCGILVRAY, JOHN, born 1760 on Skye, husband of Sarah Buchanan, from Skye, and son Alexander born 1788 on Skye, husband of Mary Elizabeth McLeod, born 1794 on Skye, emigrated to North Carolina around 1803, settled in Richmond County, N.C. [CS.255]

MCGILVRAE, JOHN, tenant of Ardellum, Ulva, in 1824. [NRS.GD174.1140.9]

MCGILVARY, MALCOLM, born 1787 on Skye, emigrated to North Carolina by 1811, died in Richmond County, North Carolina, by January 1822, husband of Mary....., born 1785 on Skye, died in Barbour County, Alabama, by 1870. [CS.255]

MCGILLVRAY, MALCOLM, on Raasay, accused of deforcement in 1838. [NRS.AD14.38.16]

MCGILVARY, MARTIN, born 1802 on Skye, son of Daniel McGilvary and his wife Catherine, died in Alabama between 1855 and 1860. [CS.254]

MCGILLIVRAY, WILLIAM, born 1764 at Peine an Ghael, Mull, formerly in Montreal, died in London on 16 October 1825. [GM.95.380]

MCGLACHAN, DONALD, born 1787, with Catherine born 1807, Angus born 1833, Alexander born 1835, Ann born 1837, Flora born 1839, Donald born 1841, and Neil born 1848, from North Uist, emigrated via Greenock aboard the <u>Cashmere of Glasgow</u> bound for Quebec in 1849. [NRS.GD221.4011.53]

MCGLASHAN, ALEXANDER, born 1795, Janet born 1796, John born 1825, Angus born 1827, Alexander born 1829, Donald born 1831, Lachlan born 1833, Donald born 1836, Mary born 1836, and Catherine born 1838, from North Uist, emigrated via

Greenock aboard the <u>Waterhen of London</u> bound for Quebec in 1849. [NRS.GD221.4435]

MCGLASHAN, JOHN, son of the late Dugald McGlashan, in Port Charron, Lismore, servant to Duncan McLullich tenant in Auchcarron, was accused of assault in 1819. [NRS.AD14.19.234]

MCGLASHAN, NEIL, born 1790, Euphemia born 1791, Ewen born 1826, Ann born 1828, Christy born 1831, Alexander born 1836, Allan born 1838, Donald born 1840, and Mary born 1842, from North Uist, emigrated via Greenock aboard the <u>Cashmere of Glasgow</u> bound for Quebec in 1849. [NRS.GD221.4011.53]

MCGREGOR, ALEXANDER, born 1770, late tenant in Crogan, died on 23 May 1833. [Killean, Loch Spelve, gravestone]

MCGREGOR, ALEXANDER, minister of Kilmuir, Skye, a letter, 1844. [NRS.GD1.537.2]

MCGREGOR, DUGALD, born 1795, died at Lochdonhead on 24 October 1864, husband of Catherine, daughter of John McDonald a farmer at Kilninian. [Killean, Loch Spelve, Mull, gravestone]

MACGREGOR, GREGOR, born 16 August 1787, minister of Lismore for 48 years, died 18 May 1885, his wife Mary born 1815, died 6 January 1871. [Lismore gravestone]

MCGREGOR, JOHN, born 1778, died at Port Ramsay in June 1826. [Lismore gravestone]

MCGREGOR, JOHN, born 1808, from North Uist, emigrated via Greenock aboard the <u>Waterhen of London</u> bound for Quebec in 1849. [NRS.GD221.4435]

MCGREGOR, JOHN, born 1817, Mary born 1819, Malcolm born 1842, Mary born 1845, Donald born 1847, and Duncan born

1850, from Moiven, emigrated via Liverpool aboard the Marmion bound for Moreton Bay, Australia, on 28 August 1852. [NRS.HD4/5]

MCGREGOR, MALCOLM, son of Duncan McGregor on Lismore, a mariner in Charleston, South Carolina, probate 1 October 1793, S.C.

MCGRIGOR, DONALD, a fisherman on Tanera, a letter, 1836. [NRS.AF.1.38]

MCGUGAN, JOHN, in Cnochnanerdach, Gigha, 1841. [NRS.SC50.5.1841.60]

MACHECTOR, ALEXANDER, with wife Eunice McKinnon, and children Lachlan, Donald, Malcolm, Christy, and Mary, from Muck, emigrated to Cape Breton Island in 1826. [CG]

MCILLIVAOIL, alias MCMILLAN, ALEXANDER, from Canna, guilty of shop-breaking, sentenced to be transported for fourteen years, at Inveraray on 13 September 1811. [SM.83.10/790]

MCILLVORY, JOHN BANE, in Ulva, an inventory, [NRS.CC12.5.1.4]

MCINDOER, DUNCAN, a farmer of Airidh-Ghuairidh, Mull, from 1830 until he was evicted in 1854. [Royal Commission, Highlands and Islands, a letter, pp.836]

MCINDOER, ELIZABETH, relict of Neil McCaffer messenger in Kilchoman, Islay, petitions in 1801. [NRS.CC12.6.7.4/5]

MCINNES, ALEXANDER, born 1812, Sarah born 1814, Christy , born 1822, William born 1834, Catherine born 1836, Ann born 1838, Donald born 1842, Neil born 1844, Samuel born 1846, and Alexander born 1849, from Trumpan, Waternish, Skye, emigrated via Liverpool aboard the Araminta bound for Geelong, Australia, on 20 June 1852. [NRS.HD4/5]

MCINNES, ALEXANDER, born 1819, died 16 November 1826, son of Duncan McInnes, tenant in Balicrach, and his wife Anne Fletcher. [Kilmore Dervaig gravestone, Mull]

MCINNIS, ANGUS, born 15 February 1785 on Jura, died in North Carolina on 21 October 1849. [Longstreet gravestone, Fort Bragg, Hoke County, N.C.]

MCINNES, ANGUS, with Margaret and children Mary and Angus, from Skye aboard the Malay bound for Sydney, Nova Scotia, in 1830. [NSARM.RG1.67/19]

MCINNES, ANGUS, born 1809, Catherine born 1812, Flora born 1831, Malcolm born 1836, Neil born 1838, Ewan born 1840, John born 1842, and Donald born 1845, from Borhaig, Skye, emigrated via Liverpool aboard the Allison bound for Melbourne, Australia, on 13 September 1852. [NRS.HD4/5]

MCINNES, CHARLES, born 1842, from Islay, emigrated via Glasgow on board the Damascus bound for Toronto, Canada, on 28 June 1862. [JRK]

MCINNES, or MACKINNON, DONALD, born 1797, a labourer in Scarristermore, Harris, accused of theft in 1822. [NRS.AD14.22.244]

MCINNES, DONALD, born 1834, from Islay, emigrated via Glasgow on board the Damascus bound for Toronto, Canada, on 28 June 1862. [JRK]

MCINNES, DUNCAN, son of Angus McInnes [1791-1887] and his wife Ann McColl, settled in Australia. [Isla Munda gravestone]

MCINNES, DUNCAN, born 1803, Marion born 1807, Ann born 1828, John born 1829, Christy born 1831, Malcolm born 1833, Niel born 1837, and Angus born 1839, from Hash, emigrated via Liverpool aboard the Allison bound for Melbourne, Australia, on 13 September 1852. [NRS.HD4/5]

MCINNES, DUNCAN, tenant of Aboss, Ulva, in 1824. [NRS.GD174.1140.9]

MCINNES, FINLEY, born 1807, Flora born 1814, John born 1828, Neil born 1835, Duncan born 1840, and Charles born 1847, from Crisipoll, emigrated via Liverpool aboard the Marmion bound for Moreton Bay, Australia, on 28 August 1852. [NRS.HD4/5]

MCINNES, JOHN, with Flora, from Skye aboard the Malay bound for Sydney, Nova Scotia, in 1830. [NSARM.RG1.67/19]

MCINNIS, JOHN, was accused of theft from the Moira of Tarbert in the Bay of Portree, Skye, trial, 1837. [NRS.JC26.1837.94]

MCINNES, JOHN, born 1808, Ann born 1808, Peter born 1828, Janet born 1826, Donald born 1830, Archibald born 1830, John born 1834, Mary born 1836, Sally born 1838, Anne born 1841, Dugald born 1843, and Alexander born 1846, from Iona, emigrated via Liverpool aboard the Marmion bound for Moreton Bay, Australia, on 28 August 1852. [NRS.HD4/5]

MCINNES, JOHN, born 1817, Jane born 1822, Margaret born 1846, Donald born 1848, and Jessie born 1851, from Balnagowan, [Baile nan Gobhainn], Lismore, emigrated via Liverpool aboard the Allison bound for Melbourne, Australia, on 13 September 1852. [NRS.HD4/5]

MCINNES, LACHLAN, born 1805, Marion born 1813, Donald born 1837, Flora born 1839, Finlay born 1841, John born 1843, Donald born 1844, Christy born 1846, from North Uist, emigrated via Greenock aboard the Cashmere of Glasgow bound for Quebec in 1849. [NRS.GD221.4011.53]

MCINNES, MALCOLM, with Marion and children Marion, Neil and Kit, from Skye aboard the Malay bound for Sydney, Nova Scotia, in 1830. [NSARM.RG1.67/19]

MCINNES, MARGARET, born 1819, daughter of Donald McInnes in Dabbil, North Uist, 1832. [NRS.JC26.1832.123]

MCINNES, MARION, a servant in Carsaig, Mull, 1827. [NRS.GD174.1628.447]

MCINNES, MARY, born 1805, John born 1828, Mary born 1824, Lachlan born 1834, Catherine born 1838, Marion born 1831, Anne born 1842, Anne born 1840, from Scullimas, [Sgulmus], Skye, emigrated via Liverpool aboard the Araminta bound for Geelong, Australia, on 20 June 1852. [NRS.HD4/5]

MCINNES, MARY, born 1814, Angus born 1835, and John born 1838, from Camass Cros, Skye, emigrated via Liverpool aboard the Arabian bound for Victoria, Australia, on 27 October 1852. [NRS.HD4/5]

MCINNES, MILES, with Mary and children Mary, Christy, John, and Flora, from Skye aboard the Malay bound for Sydney, Nova Scotia, in 1830. [NSARM.RG1.67/19]

MCINNES, NEIL, born 1812, Barbara born 1814, Margaret born 1836, Flora born 1839, Ann born 1840, Mary born 1848, and Anne born 1851, from Brieraig, emigrated via Liverpool aboard the Araminta bound for Geelong, Australia, on 20 June 1852. [NRS.HD4/5]

MCINNES, RONALD, born 1809, Marion born 1814, Finlay born 1843, and Angus born 1846, from North Uist, emigrated via Greenock aboard the Waterhen of London bound for Quebec in 1849. [NRS.GD221.4435]

MCINTOSH, BETSY, from Portree, Skye, applied to settle in Australia in 1854. [NRS.GD221.4437.1]

MCINTOSH, DONALD, with his sister, children of Alexander McIntosh in Mugarry, Skye, applied to settle in Australia in 1854. [NRS.GD221.4437.1]

MCINTOSH, JOHN, [died 1820], and his wife Mary McIvor, with children Murdoch and John, from Sleat, emigrated to North Carolina in 1803, settled in Moore County. [CS.259][Scotch Ever Cemetery, Moore County, N.C.]

MCINTOSH, LACHLAN, born 1817, Margaret born 1822, Christy born 1824, from Auchnalianait, emigrated via Liverpool aboard the Priscilla bound for Victoria, Australia, on 15 October 1852. [NRS.HD4/5]

MCINTOSH, MARION, born 1809, Flora born 1832, John born 1835, Kate born 1841, and Archibald born 1843, from Fangue, Sleat, emigrated via Liverpool aboard the Priscilla bound for Victoria, Australia, on 15 October 1852. [NRS.HD4/5]

MCINTOSH, Mrs M., a widow with four sons and three daughters, from Lealt, Skye, applied to emigrate to Australia in 1854. [NRS.GD221.4437.1]

MCINTYRE, ALEXANDER, from South Uist, emigrated via Tobermory, Mull, on board the Emperor Alexander of Aberdeen bound for Cape Breton in July 1823, landed there on 16 September 1823. [Inverness Journal, 30.1.1824]

MCINTYRE, ALEXANDER, tenant of Upper Kilvickewan, Ulva, in 1824. [NRS.GD174.1140.9]

MACINTYRE, ANGUS, born 1781, with Mary MacAulay his wife, and children Maryann, Catherine, Effie, Neil, Hector born 1815, Angus born 1817, and John born 1821,from the Western Isles, possibly emigrated on board the Harmony to Cape Breton in 1821.

MCINTYRE, ANGUS, from Benbecula, emigrated aboard the Emperor Alexander of Aberdeen, master Alexander Watt, from Tobermory, Mull, to Sydney, Cape Breton, in July 1823., landed on 16 September 1823. [Inverness Journal, 30 January 1824]

MACINTYRE, ANGUS, from South Uist, emigrated aboard the Emperor Alexander of Aberdeen, master Alexander Watt, from Tobermory, Mull, to Sydney, Cape Breton, in July 1823, landed on 16 September 1823. [Inverness Journal, 30 January 1824]

MCINTYRE, ARCHIBALD, in Dervaig, husband of Mary McKinnon, born 1771, died in November 1818, parents of Mary born 1790, died in November 1817, and Christopher, born 1800, died 1817. [Kilmore Dervaig gravestone, Mull]

MACINTYRE, Mrs CATHERINE, from South Uist, settled in Bornish, New Middlesex, Ontario, before 1866. [NLS.Acc.6869]

MCINTYRE, CHRISTIAN, a widow in Tirlaggan, Lismore, a letter, 1830. [NRS.GD170.2572]

MCINTYRE, COLIN, born 1808, a labourer in Skeabost, Skye, accused of stealing a horse, 1830. [NRS.AD14.30.379]

MACINTYRE, DOMHNULL, born 1748, his son Iain MacIntyre born 1783, with his wife Caitriona Walker and their children Aonghas born 1808, and Seonaid Fannie born 1821; Alastair MacIntyre born 1789 son of Domhnull Macintyre, with his wife Ciorsden MacInnis and their children Domhnull, Mairi, Tormad Mor, and Griogair, from Boisdale, South Uist; also Aonghas born 1799 another son of Domhnull MacIntyre, possibly emigrated on board the Harmony to Cape Breton in 1821.

MCINTYRE, DUGALD, a joint-tenant of Auchenadeunie, Lismore, a letter to Sir Duncan Campbell of Barcaldine, his landlord, re inability to pay rent, 1824. [NRS.GD170.2349]

MCINTYRE, DUGALD, born 1779, a lime merchant in Salen, Lismore, died in January 1848. [Lismore gravestone]

MACINTYRE, DUNCAN, from Benbecula, emigrated aboard the Emperor Alexander of Aberdeen, master Alexander Watt, from Tobermory, Mull, to Sydney, Cape Breton, in July 1823., landed on 16 September 1823. [Inverness Journal, 30 January 1824]

MACINTYRE, DUNCAN, [son of Hector the son of Angus], his wife Marion McLeod, and family, were evicted from Bun na Liggie, South Uist, and sent to America in the 1840s. [SCA.DA9.43]

MACINTYRE, EFFY, from South Uist, emigrated aboard the Emperor Alexander of Aberdeen, master Alexander Watt, from Tobermory, Mull, to Sydney, Cape Breton, in July 1823., landed on 16 September 1823. [Inverness Journal, 30 January 1824]

MCINTYRE, FLORA, born 1766, with Donald born 1783, Sarah born 1786, Mary born 1788, from Tobermory, Mull, aboard the brig Humphreys bound for Prince Edward Island in 1806. [PAPEI.2702]

MCINTYRE, FLORA, died on 1 January 1858. [Kilvickeon gravestone, Mull]

MCINTYRE, FLORENCE, spouse of Archibald McLean in Ballimartin, Tiree, who died in Soroba, Tiree, a decreet, 1815. [NRS.CC12.7.13.1]

MCINTYRE, HUGH, son of Donald McIntyre ground officer of Ballegroundel, Lismore, a letter, 1831. [NRS.GD170.2580]

MCINTYRE, JOHN, born 1783 on South Uist, [Uibhist a Deas], died 18 November 1847, his wife Catherine born 1785 on South Uist, died 13 July 1857. [St Andrew's RC Cemetery, Boisdale, Cape Breton.]

MCINTYRE, Reverend JOHN, born at Kinlochlaish on Lismore, on 21 August 1750, son of John Donald McIntyre and his wife Catherine Ann Stuart, husband of Catherine Ann McCallum, emigrated from Appin to Wilmington, North Carolina, in 1791, settled in Cumberland County, N.C., a Presbyterian minister in Robeson County from 1820 to 1837, died in Hoke County, N.C., on 17 November 1852, buried in Antioch. [CS.348][St Paul's records][Hoke gravestone]; born in Scotland, aged 100, in Robeson County, N.C. [1850 Census]

MACINTYRE, JOHN, from South Uist, emigrated aboard the Emperor Alexander of Aberdeen, master Alexander Watt, from Tobermory, Mull, to Sydney, Cape Breton, in July 1823., landed on 16 September 1823. [Inverness Journal, 30 January 1824]

MCINTYRE, JOHN, born on South Uist in 1783, died 18 November 1857, husband of Catherine, born on South Uist in 1785, died 13 July 1857. [St Andrew's Cemetery, Boisdale, Cape Breton]

MCINTYRE, JOHN, born 1808, a labourer, son of Colin McIntyre in Skeabost, Skye, was accused of horse stealing in Argyll, 1830. [NRS.AD14.30.379]

MCINTYRE, JOHN, in Kilinne, Lismore, a petition, 1830. [NRS.GD170.564.19]

MCINTYRE, JOHN, and his daughter from Portree, Skye, applied to emigrate to Australia in 1854. [NRS.GD221.4437.1]

MACINTYRE, MICHAEL, his wife Marion McLeod, and family, were evicted from Bun na Liggie, South Uist, and sent to America in the 1840s. [SCA.DA9.43]

MCINTYRE, NICOL, born 1809, Janet born 1819, Angus born 1838, Peter born 1842, and Mary born 1846, from Torosay, emigrated via Liverpool aboard the Panama bound for Van Diemen's Land, Australia, on 8 January 1853. [NRS.HD4/5]

MCINTYRE, NORMAN, born 1809, Mary born 1809, Innes born 1834, Marion 1837, Peggy born 1839, from North Uist, emigrated via Greenock aboard the Waterhen of London bound for Quebec in 1849. [NRS.GD221.4435]

MCINTYRE, PETER, a butcher in Bowmore, Islay, 1845. [NRS.SC50.5.1845.3]

MCINTYRE, ROBERT, on Barra, a letter dated 16 February 1800. [NRS.NRAS.2177, bundle 1506]

MCINTYRE, RODERICK, born on South Uist in 1821, died on 18 April 1883. [St Andrew's Cemetery, Boisdale, Cape Breton]

MACINTYRE, RONALD, from South Uist, emigrated aboard the Emperor Alexander of Aberdeen, master Alexander Watt, from Tobermory, Mull, to Sydney, Cape Breton, in July 1823., landed on 16 September 1823. [Inverness Journal, 30 January 1824]

MCISAAC, ANN, from Shuna, [Eilean Seona], emigrated via Druimindarroch on board the Lucy bound for Prince Edward Island in July 1790. [SCA]

MCISAAC,........., with children Flory, Mary, Peggy, Flora, and Donald, from Rum, emigrated via Leith on board the St Lawrence of Newcastle to Port Hawkesbury, Cape Breton, in 1828. [PANS.M6.100]

MCIVER, COLIN, sr., a merchant in Stornaway, [Steornabhagh], Lewis, was appointed as an attorney of John McIver a merchant in Alexandria, Virginia, on 19 December 1788. [NRS.RD2.254.922]

MCIVER, Reverend COLIN, born in Stornaway, Lewis, on 9 March 1781, settled in Fayetteville, North Carolina, as a teacher in 1809, died there in 1850. ['The Story of Fayetteville']

MCIVER, JOHN, the elder, a merchant in Stornaway, Lewis, was appointed as an attorney of John McIver a merchant in Alexandria, Virginia, on 19 December 1788. [NRS.RD2.254.922]

MCIVOR, JOHN, born 1794 in Stornaway, Lewis, died 1877. [United Church cemetery, Fox Harbour, Cumberland County, Nova Scotia]

MCIVER, MALCOLM, born 1800 on Lewis, died 21 September 1868. [Little Narrows cemetery, Victoria County, Nova Scotia]

MCIVER, NANCY, born 1787 on Skye, emigrated to America in 1802, died 24 October 1877, buried in Union Cemetery, Carthage, Moore County, North Carolina. [Moore County gravestone]

MCKAY, ALEXANDER, born 1820, Christy born 1826, Donald born 1847, Marion born 1849, and Christy born 1851, from Glasphen, emigrated via Liverpool aboard the Allison bound for Melbourne, Australia, on 13 September 1852. [NRS.HD4/5]

MCKAY, ALLAN, born around 1816, from Rum, emigrated via Leith on board the St Lawrence of Newcastle to Port Hawkesbury, Cape Breton, in 1828. [PANS.M6.100]

MACKAY, ANGUS, born 1834, shepherd to George Mitchell tacksman of Fimsgary, Uig, Lewis, accused of sheep stealing in 1850. [NRS.AD14.50.256]

MCKAY, ANN, born around 1788, with Duncan born 1808, Mary born 1803, and Neil born 1810, from Rum, emigrated via Leith on board the St Lawrence of Newcastle to Port Hawkesbury, Cape Breton, in 1828. [PANS.M6.100]

MCKAY, CATHERINE, from Rum, emigrated via Leith on board the St Lawrence of Newcastle to Port Hawkesbury, Cape Breton, in 1828. [PANS.M6.100]

MCKAY, DONALD, born 1763, from Rum, emigrated via Leith on board the St Lawrence of Newcastle to Port Hawkesbury, Cape Breton, in 1828. [PANS.M6.100]

MCKAY, DONALD, born 1794, from Uig, Lewis, emigrated to the Red River settlement in 1811. [PAC.M155.145]

MCKAY, GILCHRIST, a labourer, son of John McKay a tenant farmer in Strathaird, Skye, 1831. [NRS.JC26.1831.379]

MCKAY, JOHN, born 1809, from Rum, emigrated via Leith on board the St Lawrence of Newcastle to Port Hawkesbury, Cape Breton, in 1828. [PANS.M6.100]

MCKAY, LACHLAN, born 1809, from Rum, emigrated via Leith on board the St Lawrence of Newcastle to Port Hawkesbury, Cape Breton, in 1828. [PANS.M6.100]

MCKAY, MALCOLM, born in Uig, Lewis, in 1803, died 30 December 1887, husband of Margaret born in Uig, Lewis, settled in Cape Breton in 1825. [Little Narrows Cemetery, Victoria County, Nova Scotia]

MCKAY, NEIL, born 1768, wife Mary born 1771, Mary born 1793, Donald born 1795, Jessie born 1795, Flory born 1798, John born 1802, Christina born 1807, and Ann, from Rum, emigrated via Leith aboard the St Lawrence of Newcastle bound for Port Hawkesbury, Cape Breton, in 1828. [PANS.M6-100]

MCKAY, JOHN, born 1809, from Rum, emigrated via Leith on board the St Lawrence of Newcastle to Port Hawkesbury, Cape Breton, in 1828. [PANS.M6.100]

MACKAY, NEILL, tenant in Ballachlaven, Islay, versus Ronald McKay and Archibald McKay in Ballachlaven, in June 1831. [NRS.CS46.1831.128]

MCKAY, PETER, born 1793, with wife Flora born 1798, Lachlan born 1823, Donald born 1825, Angus born 1826, and John an infant, from Rum, emigrated via Leith aboard the St Lawrence of Newcastle bound for Port Hawkesbury, Cape Breton, in 1828. [PANS.M6-100]

MCKAY, JOHN, born 1809, from Rum, emigrated via Leith on board the St Lawrence of Newcastle to Port Hawkesbury, Cape Breton, in 1828. [PANS.M6.100]

MACKAY, RODERICK, in Valtos, Uig, Lewis, accused of theft in 1847. [NRS.AD14.47.526]

MCKEAGAN, ALEXANDER, born 1790, Mary born 1791, Angus born 1824, and John born 1829, from North Uist, emigrated via Greenock aboard the Waterhen of London bound for Quebec in 1849. [NRS.GD221.4435]

MCKEARY, JOHN, born 1789, Christy born 1799, Christy born 1828, Ann born 1830, Alexander born 1832, Archibald born 1834, Catherine born 1842, from North Uist, emigrated via Greenock aboard the Waterhen of London bound for Quebec in 1849. [NRS.GD221.4435]

MCKECHNIE, JOHN, born 1840, from Islay, emigrated via Glasgow on board the Damascus bound for Toronto, Canada, on 28 June 1862. [JRK]

MCKECHNIE, MALCOLM, born 1824, with his wife born 1836, Angus born 1854, Peter born 1856, and Malcolm born 1856, from Islay, emigrated via Glasgow on board the Damascus bound for Toronto, Canada, on 28 June 1862. [JRK]

MACKEICH, ARCHIBALD, farmer of South Cambeg, Gigha, [Giogha], 1850. [NRS.SC50.5.1850.10]

MACKELLAR, DOUGAL, husband of Sarah who died in 1814. [Kilvickeon gravestone, Mull]

MACKELLAR, D., died in February 1832. [Kilvickeon gravestone]

MACKELLAR, DUGALD, in Scour, Ross of Mull, Mull, a letter from James MacGillivray in Vaughen township, Canada West, dated 2 December 1849. [NRS.NRAS.1209.1803]

MCKENZIE, ALEXANDER, born on Lewis [Leodhas], in 1784, died 1851, husband of Barbara, born on Lewis in 1795, died 1869. [Mackenzie Cemetery North Shore, Malagash, Cumberland County, Nova Scotia]

PEOPLE OF THE HEBRIDES, 1800-1850

MCKENZIE, ALEXANDER, born 1792, John born 1834, Duncan born 1844, William born 1847, Janet born 1836, and Flora born 1838, from Islay, emigrated via Glasgow on board the Damascus bound for Toronto, Canada, on 28 June 1862. [JRK]

MACKENZIE, ALEXANDER, born on Lewis in 1797, died in 1859. [United Church Cemetery, Malagash, Cumberland County, Nova Scotia]

MCKENZIE, ALEXANDER, in Tarbert, Harris, a decreet, 1829. [NRS.CS44.171.10]

MCKENZIE, ALEXANDER, born 1817, Marion born 1824, and Donald an infant, from Uig, emigrated via Liverpool aboard the Priscilla bound for Victoria, Australia, on 15 October 1852. [NRS.HD4/5]

MACKENZIE, ALLAN, born 1786 in the parish of Lochs, Lewis, [Leodhas], died in 1850. [Mackenzie Cemetery, North Shore, Malagash, Cumberland County, Nova Scotia]

MCKENZIE, ALLAN, born 1826, from North Uist, [Uibhist], emigrated via Greenock aboard the Waterhen of London bound for Quebec in 1849. [NRS.GD221.4435]

MCKENZIE, ANDREW, born 1795, with Mary born 1799, Euphemia born 1827, Elspet born 1829, John born 1830, James born 1833, and Archibald born 1836, from North Uist, emigrated via Greenock aboard the Waterhen of London bound for Quebec in 1849. [NRS.GD221.4435]

MCKENZIE, Mrs CHRISTINA, from St Kilda, wife of John McKenzie, died in North Carolina on 24 September 1848. [Cross Creek gravestone, N.C.]

MCKENZIE, DONALD, with Anne and children Peggy, Duncan, and Alexander, from Skye [Sgiathaach], aboard the Malay bound for Sydney, Nova Scotia, in 1830. [NSARM.RG1.67/19]

MCKENZIE, DONALD, born 1817, Effy born 1818, Kenneth born 1846, and Norman born 1851, from Garlish, emigrated via Liverpool aboard the Araminta bound for Geelong, Australia, on 20 June 1852. [NRS.HD4/5]

MCKENZIE, DONALD, with his sister, from Sconser, Skye, emigrated on board the Edward Johnston to Australia in 1854. [NRS.GD221.4437.1]

MCKENZIE, DUNCAN, born 1827, Christy born 1828, Mary born 1850, from Coliemore, [Coillemor], emigrated via Liverpool aboard the Priscilla bound for Victoria, Australia, on 15 October 1852. [NRS.HD4/5]

MCKENZIE, ERIC, and his wife Christy Morison, in Handa, [Eilean Shannda], were parents of Donald baptised there in 1829, and Harry baptised there in 1831. [HS.20.5]

MCKENZIE, FLORA, born 1826, and Ann born 1836, from Sconsay, emigrated via Liverpool aboard the Arabian bound for Victoria, Australia, on 27 October 1852. [NRS.HD4/5]

MCKENZIE, FLORY, born 1810, from Rum, emigrated via Leith on board the St Lawrence of Newcastle to Port Hawkesbury, Cape Breton, in 1828. [PANS.M6.100]

MCKENZIE, GEORGE, born 1800 on Lewis, [Leodhas], died 1875, husband of Ellen, born 1820 on Lewis, died 1890. [Mackenzie Cemetery North Shore, Malagash, Cumberland County, Nova Scotia]

MACKENZIE, JOHN, born 1762 on Lewis, emigrated to Nova Scotia in 1811, died 1849. [Mackenzie Cemetery North Shore, Malagash, Cumberland County, Nova Scotia]

MACKENZIE, JOHN, born 1791 on Lewis, died 1863. [Mackenzie Cemetery North Shore, Malagash, Cumberland County, Nova Scotia]

MCKENZIE, JOHN KENNETH, born in Stornaway, Lewis, [Leodhas], emigrated to Nova Scotia in 1824, minister in Pictou, N.S., from 1824 until his death in 1838. [History of the Presbyterian Church, Toronto. 1885]

MCKENZIE, JOHN, with Kate, from Skye aboard the Malay bound for Sydney, Nova Scotia, in 1830. [NSARM.RG1.67/19]

MCKENZIE, JOHN, born 1831, Jane born 1833, Mary born 1830, Murdoch born 1843, from Stronsay, emigrated via Liverpool aboard the Priscilla bound for Victoria, Australia, on 15 October 1852. [NRS.HD4/5]

MCKENZIE, JOHN, born 1815, Mary born 1820, Archibald born 1839, Kenneth born 1841, Mary born 1845, Malcolm born 1849, and Donald born 1851, emigrated via Liverpool aboard the Priscilla bound for Victoria, Australia, on 15 October 1852. [NRS.HD4/5]

MCKENZIE, JOHN, born 1822, Marion born 1825, Ann born 1842, and Mary an infant, from Struan [Sruthan] emigrated via Liverpool aboard the Priscilla bound for Victoria, Australia, on 15 October 1852. [NRS.HD4/5]

MCKENZIE, KENNETH, born 1814, Catherine born 1815, Flora born 1832, John born 1836, Ann born 1838, Duncan born 1840, Mary born 1847, Flora born 1849 and Sarah born 1851, from Sconser, Skye, [Sgiathanach], emigrated via Liverpool aboard the Araminta bound for Geelong, Australia, on 26 May 1852. [NRS.HD4/5]

MCKENZIE, MALCOLM, with Christy, and children Roderick, John and Flora, from Skye aboard the Malay bound for Sydney, Nova Scotia, in 1830. [NSARM.RG1.67/19]

MCKENZIE, Mrs MARY, a widow with two sons, from Collimore, Skye, applied to emigrate to Australia in 1854. [NRS.GD221.4437.1]

MCKENZIE, MURDOCH, in Bosta, Lewis, a victim of crime in 1837. [NRS.AD14.37.6]

MCKENZIE, MURDOCH, born 1823, Catharine born 1823, John born 1844, Mary born 1846, Kenneth born 1848, and Ann born 1851, from Collymore, emigrated via Liverpool aboard the Priscilla bound for Victoria, Australia, on 15 October 1852. [NRS.HD4/5]

MCKENZIE, MURDOCH, born 1789, Catherine born 1789, Christy born 1812, John born 1832, and Mary born 1834, from Coliemore [Coillemore], emigrated via Liverpool aboard the Priscilla bound for Victoria, Australia, on 15 October 1852. [NRS.HD4/5]

MCKENZIE, NEIL, born 1792, John born 1823, Ann born 1827, Frank born 1829, and Kate born 1832, from Sconsay, emigrated via Liverpool aboard the Priscilla bound for Victoria, Australia, on 15 October 1852. [NRS.HD4/5]

MCKEWEN, DONALD, born 1791, a labourer, Allan born 1795, Angus born 1800, Mary born 1789, Isabella born 1798, and Effie born 1800, from Kilfinichen, Mull, emigrated to Hudson Bay in 1812. [NAC.SP[C1].294, 558-561]

MCKINLAY, FLORA, born 1827 in Lewis, wife of Richard C. Smith, died on 10 November 1854, buried in the British Cemetery, Funchal, Madeira.

MCKINNISON, ARCHIBALD, born 1799, Elizabeth born 1813, Neil born 1842, from North Uist, emigrated via Greenock aboard the Waterhen of London bound for Quebec in 1849. [NRS.GD221.4435]

MCKINNON, ALEXANDER, tenant of Ardellum, Ulva, in 1824. [NRS.GD174.1140.9]

MCKINNON, ALEXANDER, in Strath, Skye, a letter, 1825. [NRS.GD23.6.605]

MCKINNON, ALEXANDER, born 1788, died 3 January 1827. [Kilviceuen gravestone, Ulva]

MCKINNON, ALLEN, born 1773 on Mull, died in Caledon, Peel County, Ontario, on 15 August 1860; his wife Mary McQuarrie, born 1793 on Mull, died 23 February 1884. [Caledon gravestone]

MCKINNON, ANGUS, born 1787, a feuar in Tobermory, died 26 February 1839. [Tobermory gravestone]

MCKINNON, ANN, born 1768, from Rum, emigrated via Leith on board the St Lawrence of Newcastle to Port Hawkesbury, Cape Breton, in 1828. [PANS.M6.100]

MCKINNON, ARCHIBALD, born 1772, his wife Marion McLean born 1776, Mary born 1802 and Alexander an infant, from Torinbeg, Kilfinichen, Mull, emigrated to Hudson Bay in 1812. [NAC.SP[C1], 294, 558-561]

MCKINNON, ARCHIBALD, tenant of Culinish, Ulva, in 1824. [NRS.GD174.1140.9]

MCKINNON, ARCHIBALD, born 1800, from Rum, emigrated via Leith on board the St Lawrence of Newcastle to Port Hawkesbury, Cape Breton, in 1828. [PANS.M6.100]

MCKINNON, ARCHIBALD, born 1815, Mary born 1816, Neil born 1836, Christy born 1839, John born 1841, Catherine born 1845, Godfrey born 1847, and sister Mary born 1828, from Camuscross, Skye, emigrated via Liverpool aboard the Araminta bound for Geelong, Australia, on 20 June 1852. [NRS.HD4/5]

MCKINNON, CHARLES, born 1778 on Sleat, died in North Carolina on 7 May 1816, buried in Murchison Cemetery, North Carolina. [Murchison gravestone]

MCKINNON, CHARLES, born 1789 in Strath, Skye, died in South Carolina on 9 July 1833, buried in the Scotch Cemetery, Bethune, Kershaw County, S.C. [Kershaw gravestone]

MACKINNON, CHARLES FARQUHAR, born 1820 on Sleat, son of Reverend John MacKinnon and his wife Anne MacKinnon, settled in Melbourne, Australia. [F.7.183]

MCKINNON, DANIEL, born on Coll, [Cola], in 1805, died 8 December 1873. [Sardis gravestone, Cumberland County, North Carolina]

MCKINNON, DONALD, born 1760 on Mull, settled in Prince Edward Island, died at York River on 4 June 1839. [Charlottetown gravestone, PEI.]

MCKINNON, DONALD, tenant of Ardellum, Ulva, in 1824. [NRS.GD174.1140.9]

MCKINNON, DONALD, born 1780, wife Catherine born 1778, from Rum, emigrated via Leith on board the St Lawrence of Newcastle to Port Hawkesbury, Cape Breton, in 1828. [PANS.M6.100]

MCKINNON, DONALD, born 1781, wife Margaret born 1782, Jessie born 1807, Lachlin born 1808, Donald born 1812, Catherine born 1818, Angus born 1822, and Peter born 1825, from Rum, emigrated via Leith on board the St Lawrence of Newcastle to Port Hawkesbury, Cape Breton, in 1828. [PANS.M6.100]

MCKINNON, DONALD, with Christy, from Skye aboard the Malay bound for Sydney, Nova Scotia, in 1830. [NSARM.RG1.67/19]

MCKINNON, DONALD, born 1827, emigrated via Liverpool aboard the British Queen bound for Victoria on 8 January 1853. [NRS.HD4/5]

MCKINNON, DUNCAN, born 1765, wife Mary born 1770, Alexander born 1798, Ann born 1803, Lachlin born 1804, Ann born 1808, Catherine born 1813, and Donald born 1809, from Rum, emigrated via Leith on board the St Lawrence of Newcastle to Port Hawkesbury, Cape Breton, in 1828. [PANS.M6.100]

MACKINNON, DUNCAN, died 1852, husband of Mary Campbell died 1886. [Kilvickeon gravestone, Mull]

MCKINNON, FLORY, born 1788, from Rum, emigrated via Leith on board the St Lawrence of Newcastle to Port Hawkesbury, Cape Breton, in 1828. [PANS.M6.100]

MACKINNON, GODFREY BOSVILLE, born 1834 on Strath, Skye, son of Reverend John MacKinnon and his wife Anne MacKinnon, settled in Melbourne, Australia. [F.7.183]

MACKINNON, HECTOR, born 1787, died 2 May 1837. [Kilmore Dervaig gravestone, Mull]

MCKINNON, HUGH, born 1755, Catherine born 1761, Mary born 1786, Neal born 1787, John born 1792, Malcolm born 1794, Catherine born 1796, Angus born 1798, Elizabeth born 1800, Roderick born 1804, from Tobermory, Mull, [Tobar Mhoire, Muile], aboard the brig Humphreys bound for Prince Edward Island in 1806. [PAPEI.2702]

MCKINNON, JOHN, a tenant from Cleadale, Eigg, [Cleadail, Eige], with family, emigrated via Arisaig aboard The British Queen of Greenock to Quebec in 1790. [NAC.RG4A1.48.15874-5]

MCKINNON, J., tenant of Berniss, Ulva, in 1824. [NRS.GD174.1140.9]

MCKINNON, JOHN, tenant of Culinish, Ulva, in 1824. [NRS.GD174.1140.9]

MACKINNON, JOHN, born 1773, tenant in Brolas, died 17 March 1827. [Killunaig gravestone, Mull]

MCKINNON, JOHN, born 1780, wife Ann born 1783, Bell born 1808, Donald born 1810, and Mary born 1813, from Rum, emigrated via Leith on board the St Lawrence of Newcastle to Port Hawkesbury, Cape Breton, in 1828. [PANS.M6.100]

MCKINNON, JOHN, born 1798, from Rum, emigrated via Leith on board the St Lawrence of Newcastle to Port Hawkesbury, Cape Breton, in 1828. [PANS.M6.100]

MCKINNON, JOHN, with Flora and children John, Christy, and Alexander, from Skye aboard the Malay bound for Sydney, Nova Scotia, in 1830. [NSARM.RG1.67/19]

MACKINNON, JOHN, born 1790, Janet born 1790, Marion born 1829, and John born 1839, from Scalamas, emigrated via Liverpool aboard the Allison bound for Melbourne, Australia, on 13 September 1852. [NRS.HD4/5]

MACKINNON, JOHN, [son of Thormaid, son of Neil, son of John the fair, 'mac Thormaic ic Neil ic Ian bhan'], with his wife Ann MacLennan and family, were evicted from Bun na Liggie, South Uist, and sent to America in the 1840s. [SCA.DA9.43]

MCKINNON, JOHN, born 1802, died 18 February 1843, son of Euphemia McKinnon, born 1778, died 8 August 1855. [Kilpatrick gravestone, Mull]

MCKINNON, JOHN, born 1820, Catherine born 1830, from Elgoll, Skye, [Elaghol, Sgiothanach], emigrated via Liverpool aboard the Araminta bound for Geelong, Australia, on 20 June 1852. [NRS.HD4/5]

MACKINNON, JOHN, late pensioner in Fanmore, died in December 1855, husband of Mary McLean, died November 1864. [Calgary Bay gravestone, Mull]

MCKINNON, JOHN, born 1812, Neil born 1835, Norman born 1837, Marion born 1839, and Angus born 1837, emigrated from Harris on board the Clansman bound for Australia on 13 July 1857. [NRS.GD371.241.1]

MCKINNON, LACHLAN, born 1744, in Baliograch, died August 1834, husband of Catherine McLean. [Tobermory gravestone]

MCKINNON, LAUCHLAN, a tenant from Cleadale, Eigg, emigrated via Arisaig aboard The British Queen of Greenock to Quebec in 1790. [NAC.RG4A1.48.15874-5]

MCKINNON, LAUCHLIN, born 1760 in Strath, Skye, died in South Carolina on 24 June 1834, buried in the Scotch Cemetery, Bethune, Kershaw County, S.C. [Bethune gravestone]

MCKINNON, LAUCHLIN, born 1761, Catherine born 1768, Margaret born 1798, Janet born 1800, Roderick born 1804, Duncan born 1806, from Tobermory, Mull, aboard the brig Humphreys bound for Prince Edward Island in 1806. [PAPEI.2702]

MCKINNON, LAUCHLIN, born 1794, aboard the brig Isle of Skye bound for Prince Edward Island in 1806. [PAPEI.2702]

MCKINNON, LAUCHLAN, tenant of Eolasary, Ulva, in 1824. [NRS.GD174.1140.9]

MCKINNON, LACHLAN, tenant of Culinish, Ulva, in 1824. [NRS.GD174.1140.9]

MCKINNON, LACHLIN, born 1788, wife Marion born 1783, Lachlin born 1816, Catherine born 1818, Archibald born 1820, Donald born 1822, and Mary an infant, from Rum, emigrated via Leith on board the St Lawrence of Newcastle to Port Hawkesbury, Cape Breton, in 1828. [PANS.M6.100]

MCKINNON, LACHLIN, born 1812, Ann born 1816, and Allan born 1820, from Rum, emigrated via Leith on board the St Lawrence of Newcastle to Port Hawkesbury, Cape Breton, in 1828. [PANS.M6.100]

MCKINNON, MALCOLM, born 1740, from Rum, emigrated via Leith on board the St Lawrence of Newcastle to Port Hawkesbury, Cape Breton, in 1 828. [PANS.M6.100]

MCKINNON, MALCOLM, born 1783, Christina born 1810, Catherine born 1813, John born 1815, Marian born 1818, Peggy born 1822, Flory born 1824, and Bell born 1826, from Rum, emigrated via Leith on board the St Lawrence of Newcastle to Port Hawkesbury, Cape Breton, in 1828. [PANS.M6.100]

MCKINNON, MALCOLM, born 1798, died 5 September 1856. [Tobermory gravestone]

MCKINNON, MALCOLM, born 1803, Janet born 1812, Alexander born 1845, and Kenneth born 1850, from Bernisdale, [Bearnasdal], Skye, emigrated via Liverpool aboard the Ticonderoga bound for Port Philip, Australia, on 4 August 1852. [NRS.HD4/5]

MCKINNON, MARGARET, born 1768, Flory born 1798, and Catherine born 1800, from Rum, emigrated via Leith on board the St Lawrence of Newcastle to Port Hawkesbury, Cape Breton, in 1828. [PANS.M6.100]

MCKINNON, MARGARET, born 1768, Alexander born 1800, Alyson born 1800, Jessie born 1802, John born 1807. And Catherine born 1812, from Rum, emigrated via Leith on board the St Lawrence of Newcastle to Port Hawkesbury, Cape Breton, in 1828. [PANS.M6.100]

MCKINNON, MARGARET, born 1790, from Rum, emigrated via Leith on board the St Lawrence of Newcastle to Port Hawkesbury, Cape Breton, in 1828. [PANS.M6.100]

MCKINNON, MARGARET, born 1814, Donald born 1835, Alexander born 1837, John born 1839, and John born 1848, from Hurbroda, emigrated via Liverpool on board the Allison bound for Melbourne, Australia, on 13 September 1852. [NRS.HD4/5]

MCKINNON, MARY, born 1802, Ann born 1823, John born 1825, and Flory an infant, from Rum, emigrated via Leith on board the St Lawrence of Newcastle to Port Hawkesbury, Cape Breton, in 1828. [PANS.M6.100]

MCKINNON, NEAL, born 1764, Catherine McKinnon born 1766, Donald born 1780, Mirron born 1781, Neal born 1786, Ann born 1788, Mirron born 1802, Catherine born 1805, from Tobermory, Mull, aboard the brig Humphreys bound for Prince Edward Island in 1806. [PAPEI.2702]

MCKINNON, NEIL, born 1782, wife Christina McLean born 1787, with six children, from Torinbeg, Kilfinichen, Mull, emigrated to Hudson Bay in 1812. [NAC.SP[C1], 294, 558-561]

MCKINNON, NEIL, born 1767, his wife Margery McGilvra born 1772, from Glen Baire, Kilfinichen, Mull, emigrated to Hudson Bay in 1812. [NAC.SP[C1], 294, 558-561]

MACKINNON, NIALL, his wife Mairi MacPhee, and children Catriona, Raonai, Gilleasbuig, Domhnull and Alasdair, from Allasdale, Barra, possibly emigrated on board the Harmony to Cape Breton in 1821.

MCKINNON, NEIL, with Marion and children Malcolm, Mary, Kate, and Margaret, from Skye aboard the Malay bound for Sydney, Nova Scotia, in 1830. [NSARM.RG1.67/19]

MCKINNON, NEIL, born 1797, Christy born 1828, Elizabeth born 1830, Rachel born 1832, Rory born 1834, and Alexander born 1840, from Colliemore, emigrated via Liverpool aboard the Priscilla bound for Victoria, Australia, on 15 October 1852. [NRS.HD4/5]

MCKINNON, NEIL, born 1809, Christianna born 1814, Jane born 1832, Mary born 1834, Hugh born 1836, John born 1838, Dougald born 1840, Christianna born 1844, and Juliet born 1846, from Tobermory, Mull, emigrated via Liverpool aboard the Panama bound for Van Diemen's Land, Australia, on 8 January 1853. [NRS.HD4/5]

MCKINNON, NIEL, born 1814, Catherine born 1817, Susan born 1843, Ewen born 1845, and Peggy born 1845, from Breakish [Breacais] Skye, emigrated via Liverpool aboard the Allison bound for Melbourne, Australia, on 13 September 1852. [NRS.HD4/5]

MCKINNON, PEGGY, born 1808, Flory born 1811, Mary born 1815, Catherine born 1813, and Archibald born 1818, from Rum, emigrated via Leith on board the St Lawrence of Newcastle to Port Hawkesbury, Cape Breton, in 1828. [PANS.M6.100]

MCKINNON, RODERICK, born 1817, Flora born 1812, Marion born 1836, John born 1838, and Peggy born 1840, from Tote, Skye, emigrated via Glasgow aboard the Georgiana bound for Port Philip, Australia, on 13 July 1852. [NRS.HD4/5]

MACKINNON, RUAIRIDH, son of Iain Og MacKinnon and his wife Margaret MacNeil on Barra, his brother Gilleasbuig MacKinnon with his wife Marion MacDonald and their children Mairi born 1816, Eachann, Aonghas, and Anna; Murchadh, Ruairidh's brother, with Mairi MacNeil his wife and children Eachann and Alasdair; Ruairidh's sisters Mairi, Anna, Mor, and Caitriona; also his brother Eachenn Beag MacKinnon with his wife Mairi MacNeil, possibly emigrated on board the Harmony to Cape Breton in 1821.

MCLACHLAN, ALEXANDER, principal coast officer at Tobermory, Mull, in 1845. [NRS.SC505.1845.23]

MCLACHLAN, DONALD, born 1746, 'one of the first feuars here', died 11 November 1823, husband of Ann McGregor, died 1836, parents of Dougald born 1791, a merchant in Tobermory, died 14 June 1828, and Alexander born 1783, died 10 January 1851. [Tobermory gravestone]

MCLACHLAN, DUNCAN, in Scorybeck, Skye, victim of a crime in 1837. [NRS.AD14.37.35]

MCLACHLAN, JOHN, a whisky distiller at Seanghairt, Islay, in 1801, and at Keppolsmore, Islay, in 1818. [NRS.JP36.5.46]

MCLACHLAN, MARGARET, wife of Dugald McLachlan [1785-1868] a tailor in Tobermory, Mull, in 1820. [M.398]

MCLACHLAN, MARGARET, died 14 July 1842. [Kilpatrick Duart gravestone, Torosay]

MCLACHLAN, PETER, father of Duncan born 1820, died 11 February 1856, and of John, born 1822, died 28 February 1856. [Killean, Loch Spelve, gravestone, Mull]

MACLAINE, ALLAN, tacksman of Scalasdale, 1799. [NRS.GD174.209.16]

MACLAINE, ARCHIBALD, a servant of Lauchlan MacLaine in 1824. [M.315]

MACLAINE, CHARLES, a tenant of Garmony, Mull, was evicted in 1800. [M.283]

MACLAINE, HECTOR, sr., a tenant of Garmony, Mull, was evicted in 1800. [M.283]

MACLAINE, HECTOR, jr., a tenant of Garmony, Mull, was evicted in 1800. [M.283]

MACLAINE, HUGH, a tenant of Garmony, Mull, was evicted in 1800. [M.283]

MACLAINE, JOHN, tacksman of Tiroran, Mull, emigrated around 1816. [M.195]

MACLAINE, JOHN, born 1770, tenant in Ardellim of Ulva, died 22 June 1837. [Kilviceuen gravestone, Ulva]

MACLAINE, MURDOCH, of Lochbuie, Mull, [Locha Buidhe, Muile], letters, 1826-1832. [NRS.GD174.1677/1879]

MCLANE, ANGUS, born 1751, Ann born 1756, Christy born 1788, John born 1790, James born 1792, Mary born 1794, Donald born 1796, from Tobermory, Mull, aboard the brig Humphreys bound for Prince Edward Island in 1806. [PAPEI.2702]

MCLAREN, JOHN, a mason in Craignure, Mull, [Creag an Iubhair, Muile], with Janet his wife and five children, applied to emigrate to Canada in 1815. [TNA.CO385.2]

MCLAUCHLAN, JOHN, a tenant in Portcharron, Lismore, a petition, 1831. [NRS.GD170.564.23]

MCLEA, JOHN, born 1806, Flora born 1806, Mary born 1833, Donald born 1843, and James born 1844, from Waterloo, Skye, emigrated via Liverpool aboard the Allison bound for Melbourne, Australia, on 13 September 1852. [NRS.HD4/5]

MCLEAN, ALEXANDER, of Coll, and his son Hugh McLean, a bond re the purchase of the island of Muck on 4 June 1813. [NRS.GD201.5.285]

MCLEAN, ALEXANDER, born 1783, died 13 December 1813, [Torloisk gravestone, Mull]

MCLEAN, ALEXANDER, born 1802, from Rum, emigrated via Leith on board the St Lawrence of Newcastle to Port Hawkesbury, Cape Breton, in 1828. [PANS.M6.100]

MCLEAN, ALEXANDER, a fisherman in Cladart, Kilchoman, Islay, was accused of plundering a wreck, in 1821. [NRS.AD14.21.166]

MCLEAN, ALEXANDER, born 1802 on Rum, emigrated via Leith aboard the St Lawrence of Newcastle bound for Port Hawkesbury, Cape Breton, in 1828. [PANS.M6.100]

MCLEAN, ALEXANDER, born 1808, a merchant on Raasay, [Ratharsaigh], accused of deforcement in 1838. [NRS.AD14.38.16]

MCLEAN, ALEXANDER, born 1803, Catherine born 1821, Euphemia born 1829, Neil born 1836, John born 1838, Lachlan born 1843, Rachel born 1845, Donald born 1847, and Hector born 1848, from North Uist, emigrated via Greenock aboard the Cashmere of Glasgow bound for Quebec in 1849. [NRS.GD221.4011.53]

MCLEAN, ALEXANDER, born 1804, Anne born 1818, John born 1839, Ann born 1844, John born 1846, Donald born 1849, and Mary born 1851, from Stein Seabost, Skye, emigrated via Liverpool aboard the Araminta bound for Geelong, Australia, on 20 June 1852. [NRS.HD4/5]

MCLEAN, ALEXANDER, in Kyleakin, Skye, [letters, 1848. [Caol Acain, Sgaithanach], [NRS.HD10.26]

MCLEAN, ALEXANDER, born 30 June 1820 on Tiree, [Tyriodh], son of Reverend Neil McLean and his wife Isabella McDonald, emigrated to Australia. [F.4.121]

MCLEAN, ALEXANDER, born 1816, Christianna born 1820, Euphemia born 1841, Catherine born 1844, Effy born 1845, John born 1849, and Isabella born 1851, from Ard Finaing, Mull, emigrated via Liverpool aboard the Marmion bound for Moreton Bay, Australia, on 28 August 1852. [NRS.HD4/5]; a ploughman from Torosay, settled on Ardfenaig, Ross of Mull, who with his wife Cirsty and four children, who emigrated to Australia in 1852. [M.349]

MCLEAN, ALLAN, born 1770, a labourer from Mull, emigrated from Oban aboard the Clarendon of Hull, bound for Charlottetown, Prince Edward Island, in August 1808. [TNA.CO226.23]

MCLEAN, ALLAN, son of Lachlan McLean of Bunessain, [Bun Easain], Mull, a Lieutenant of the 91st Regiment, died at Vittoria, Spain, on 24 November 1813, from wounds received in the Pyrenees on 26 July 1813. [SM.76.157]

MCLEAN, ALLAN, born 1770 on Rum, with his wife Christian born 1786, and children John born 1815, Malcolm born 1817, and Flory born 1819, emigrated via Leith aboard the St Lawrence of Newcastle bound for Port Hawkesbury, Cape Breton, in 1828. [PANS.M6.100]

MCLEAN, ALLAN, born 1772, Mary born 1774, Kirsty born 1794, Mary born 1801, Hector born 1796, and Effie born 1803, emigrated to La Chine, Quebec, on board the Oughton in 1804. [PACAN. McDonell pp.105/8]

MCLEAN, ALLAN, son of John McLean, a postman and tenant of Leitier, Mull, was found guilty of letter theft and was sentenced to penal servitude in 1828. [NRS.JC26.1828.397]

MCLEAN, ANGUS, born 1748, a labourer from Mull, with daughters Mary born 1782, Ann born 1783, and grandson John McGilvray born 1805, emigrated from Oban aboard the Clarendon of Hull, bound for Charlottetown, Prince Edward Island, in August 1808. [TNA.CO226.23]

MCLEAN, ANGUS, born 1812, Effy born 1811, Mary born 1834, Donald born 1837, Janet born 1840, John born 1843, and Angus born 1850, from Stein Sleabost, Skye, emigrated via

Liverpool aboard the Araminta bound for Geelong, Australia, on 20 June 1852. [NRS.HD4/5]

MACLEAN, ANGUS, with his wife, from Tarskaveg, Skye, emigrated to Australia on board the Hornet in 1854. [NRS.GD221.4437.1]

MCLEAN, ANN, from Oransay, emigrated to La Chine, Quebec, on board the Oughton in 1804. [PACAN. McDonell pp.105/8] ,

MCLEAN, ARCHIBALD, from Torrans, Mull, formerly an officer of the New York Volunteers, died in Nashwaak, York County, New Brunswick on 18 February 1830. [St John City Gazette, 3 March 1830]

MCLEAN, ARCHIBALD, born 1787, a wright in Kilbrianan, Kilmore, Mull, Torinbeg, emigrated to Hudson Bay in 1812. [NAC.SP[C1], 294, 558-561]

MCLEAN, ARCHIBALD, born 1795, a tenant farmer of Balevulin, [Baile a'Mhuilinn], Tiree, on trial accused of theft, 1824. [NRS.AD14.24.207]

MCLEAN, ARCHIBALD, on of Duncan McLean in Portinellan, [Port Ilein], Islay, was accused of plundering a ship, in 1812. [NRS.AD14.12.92]

MCLEAN, ARCHIBALD, born 1811, Jessy born 1808, Mary born 1844, and Niel born 1850, from Ballygown [Baile a Ghobhainn] Mull, emigrated via Liverpool aboard the Marmion bound for Moreton Bay, Australia, on 28 August 1852. [NRS.HD4/5]

MCLEAN, ARCHIBALD, with two sisters, and a female relative, from Camustinaveg, Skye, applied to emigrate to Australia in 1854. [NRS.GD221.4437.1]

MCLEAN, ARCHIE, with his sister, from Glenmore, Skye, applied to emigrate to Australia in 1854. [NRS.GD221.4437.1]

MCLEAN, CATHERINE, born 1795 on Rum, emigrated via Leith aboard the St Lawrence of Newcastle bound for Port Hawkesbury, Cape Breton, in 1828. [PANS.M6.100]

MCLEAN, CHARLES, born 1773, in Ulva, died 4 October, 1843, husband of Isabella Campbell, born 1771, died in Tobermory on 21 November 1852. [Glen Aros gravestone, Mull]

MCLEAN, CHARLES, born 1787, a labourer from Mull, emigrated from Oban aboard the Clarendon of Hull, bound for Charlottetown, Prince Edward Island, in August 1808. [TNA.CO226.23]

MCLEAN, CHARLES, born 1792 on Rum, emigrated via Leith aboard the St Lawrence of Newcastle bound for Port Hawkesbury, Cape Breton, in 1828. [PANS.M6.100]

MACLEAN, COINNEACH, with Pegi Steele his wife, and sons Domhnull born 1820 and Torlach born 1821, from Frobost, South Uist, possibly emigrated on board the Harmony to Cape Breton in 1821.

MCLEAN, DONALD, born 1782, a wright, his wife Catherine Morrison born 1790, from Kilnienen, Kilmore, Mull, emigrated to Hudson Bay in 1812. [NAC.SP[C1], 294, 558-561]

MCLEAN, DONALD, born 1790, a seaman, his wife Ann McLean born 1788, from Kilfinichen, Mull, emigrated to Hudson Bay in 1812. [NAC.SP[C1], 294, 558-561]

MCLEAN, DONALD, tenant in New Ulva, 1816. [NRS.CC2.8.121.6]

MCLEAN, Reverend DONALD, on Eigg, [Eige], and his son Neil McLean a schoolmaster, letters, dated 3 March 1800, and 31 January 1831. [NRS.NRAS.2177, bundle 1506]; on Eigg, minister of the Small Isles, letters, 1803, [NRS.GD248.667.10; 656.3]

MCLEAN, DONALD, Captain of the Rum Volunteer Infantry, a letter, 1808. [NRS.GD23.6.449]

MCLEAN, DONALD, tidesman at Bowmore, [Bogha Mor], Islay, an edict of executry, 16 August 1810. [NRS.CC12.3.7-161]

MCLEAN, DONALD, postmaster at Bunessan, Mull, in 1848, husband of Margaret Dewar. [M.358]

MCLEAN, DONALD, a farmer at Leim, Gigha, in 1849. [NRS.SC50.5.1849.3]

MCLEAN, DONALD, born 1799, Flora born 1807, Donald born 1829, John born 1832, Archie born 1834, Lachlan born 1836, Mary born 1841, Alexander born 1845, Ewen born 1848, from North Uist, emigrated via Greenock aboard the Cashmere of Glasgow bound for Quebec in 1849. [NRS.GD221.4011.53]

MCLEAN, DONALD, born 1820, Marion born 1824, Mary born 1843, and Euphemia born 1847, from North Uist, emigrated via Greenock aboard the Cashmere of Glasgow bound for Quebec in 1849. [NRS.GD221.4011.53]

MCLEAN, DONALD, born 1831, died at Tobermory on 7 August 1899. [Calgary gravestone, Mull]

MCLEAN, DONALD, and Company, merchants in Kyleakin, [Caol Acain], Skye, records, 1834. 1834-1854. [NRS.CS96.1686-3003]

MACLEAN, DUNCAN, jr., a tenant of Garmony, Mull, was evicted in 1800. [M.283]

MCLEAN, DUNCAN, in Leogin, Kilmeny, [Cill Mheinidh], Islay, was accused of plundering a ship, in 1812. [NRS.AD14.12.92]

MCLEAN, DUNCAN, born 1818, Kate born 1824, Ann born 1846, Allan born 1849, and infants William and Janet, from Portree, Skye, emigrated via Liverpool aboard the Priscilla bound for Victoria, Australia, on 15 October 1852. [NRS.HD4/5]

MCLEAN, EFFY, with one son and two daughters, from Moorlands, Skye, applied to emigrate to Australia in 1854. [NRS.GD221.4437.1]

MCLEAN, FLORA, born 1823 on Jura, [Diura], died 23 April 1867 in North Carolina, buried in Union cemetery, Carthage, Moore County, North Carolina. [Moore County gravestone]

MCLEAN, GEORGE, tacksman of Highnish, Tiree, a marriage contract with Miss Duncan Malcolm Campbell in 1842. [NRS.GD1.1003.21.7]

MCLEAN, HECTOR, born 1784, with his mother Margaret McInnis, his sister Mary McLean born 1796, Alexander born 1788 a labourer, John born 1790, and Hugh born 1794, from Cambus, Kilfinichen, Mull, emigrated to Hudson Bay in 1812. [NAC.SP[C1], 294, 558-561]

MCLEAN, HECTOR, born on Tyree on 25 December 1794, died on 21 November 1877. [Riverview gravestone, Wallaceburg, Upper Canada]

MCLEAN, HECTOR, born 1796 on Rum, emigrated via Leith aboard the St Lawrence of Newcastle bound for Port Hawkesbury, Cape Breton, in 1828. [PANS.M6.100]

MACLEAN, HECTOR, born 1818 in Ballygrant, Islay, tutor and schoolmaster in Ballygrant, died 1893. [I.186]

MCLEAN, HECTOR, born 1772, tenant at Kencharair, died 6 February 1846, his wife Flora McArthur, born 1786, died 4 May 1879, parents of Donald of Gometra, born 1815, died 8 August 1871, Peter of Gometra, born 1826, died 4 May 1893, and John of Gometra, born 1835, died 17 January 1898. [Calgary Bay gravestone, Mull]

MCLEAN, HUGH, born 1779 on Rum, a farmer, with his wife Marion born 1783, and five children born between 1809 and

1824, emigrated via Leith aboard the St Lawrence of Newcastle bound for Port Hawkesbury, Cape Breton, in 1828. [PANS.M6.100]

MCLEAN, JESSIE, born 19 June 1822 on Uist, daughter of Reverend Roderick McLean and his wife Elizabeth McLeod, wife of Norman McDonald, died in Broadmeadow, New South Wales, Australia. [F7.196]

MCLEAN, JOHN, born 1724, a surgeon, died 5 March 1808, husband of Christina, born 1718, died 2 March 1808. [Kilpatrick gravestone, Mull]

MACLEAN, JOHN, born 15 April 1752, son of Reverend Alexander MacLean in Mull, an American Army officer, died in Halifax, Nova Scotia. [F.4.115]

MCLEAN, JOHN, a mariner from Islay, was naturalised in Charleston, South Carolina, on 20 April 1796. [NARA.M1183.1]

MACLEAN, JOHN, a tenant of Garmony, Mull, was evicted in 1800. [M.283]

MCLEAN, JOHN, born 1784, his wife born 1788, and two children born 1808 and 1810, from Kilbrianin, Kilmore, Mull, emigrated to Hudson Bay in 1812. [NAC.SP[C1], 294, 558-561]

MCLEAN, JOHN, born 1778, in Pingown, Kilmuir, [Cille Mhoire], Skye, was accused of sheep-stealing and housebreaking in 1838. [NRS.AD14.38.3]

MCLEAN, JOHN, a chapman in Portree, [Port Righ], Skye, accused of theft, 6 April 1801. [NRS.AC26.1801.1]

MCLEAN, JOHN, born 1771 on Mull, emigrated via Greenock on board the brig Molly bound for Wilmington, North Carolina, in 1792, settled in Robeson County, N.C., died 15 May 1846. ['Lumber River Scots']

MCLEAN, JOHN, [Iain MacGilleain], born 1787 on Tiree, emigrated to Canada in 1819, a Gaelic poet, died 1848. [HS.11.5.49]

MCLEAN, JOHN, born 1787 on Skye, emigrated to America in 1802, died 24 October 1877, buried in Union Cemetery, Moore County, North Carolina. [Moore County gravestone]

MCLEAN, JOHN, born 1792, Catherine born 1801, Mary born 1824, Margaret born 1826, Neil born 1829, Elizabeth born 1832, and Catherine born 1836, from North Uist, emigrated via Greenock aboard the Waterhen of London bound for Quebec in 1849. [NRS.GD221.4435]

MCLEAN, JOHN, [1790s-1830s], schoolmaster in Ballygown, married Margaret McCallum, [1780-1815], in 1802, parents of Alexander born 1802, John born 1808, and six others. [M.187]

MCLEAN, JOHN, in Shiaba, Ross [Headland] of Mull, a letter from his uncle Archibald MacGillivray in the township of King, Canada West, dated 20 December 1849. [NRS.NRAS.1209.1803]

MCLEAN, JOHN, born 1797, Margaret born 1827, Angus born 1830, Catherine born 1832, also John born 1833 and his wife Ann born 1834, and daughter Ann born 1850, from Clachan, emigrated via Liverpool aboard the Allison bound for Melbourne, Australia, on 13 September 1852. [NRS.HD4/5]

MCLEAN, KENNETH, from Muck, emigrated to Quebec in 1802. [LAC.MG23.183]

MCLEAN, LAUCHLAN, born 1748, a labourer from Mull, with wife Catherine born 1752, and children Flora born 1778, Hugh born 1783, Hector born 1793, John born 1796, and Euphemia born 1798, emigrated from Oban aboard the Clarendon of Hull, bound for Charlottetown, Prince Edward Island, in August 1808. [TNA.CO226.23]

MCLEAN, LACHLAN, born 1783, a labourer from Mull, with wife Ann born 1778, and daughter Janet born 1808, emigrated from Oban aboard the Clarendon of Hull, bound for Charlottetown, Prince Edward Island, in August 1808. [TNA.CO226.23]

MACLEAN, LACHLAN, of Gallanach, owner of Arivelchyne, Ardrioch and Duchorin in Mull, instigator of the evictions of Rum, 1826. [M.330]

MACLEAN, LACHLAN, died in 1847. Kilvickeon gravestone, Mull]

MCLEAN, MALCOLM, born 1797 on Jura, died 1 November 1862 in North Carolina, buried in Union cemetery, Carthage, Moore County, North Carolina. [Moore County gravestone]

MCLEAN, MARY, born 1768 on Rum, emigrated via Leith aboard the St Lawrence of Newcastle bound for Port Hawkesbury, Cape Breton, in 1828. [PANS.M6.100]

MACLEAN, MARY, a widow, a tenant of Garmony, Mull, was evicted in 1800. [M.283]

MCLEAN, MARY, in Pennycross, [Peighinn na Croise], Mull, heir to her nephew James McLean in St Mary's, Jamaica, [NRS., SH.1826]

MCLEAN, MURDOCH, born in Salen, [Sailean], Mull, on 31 January 1829, son of Reverend Duncan McLean and his wife Flora McLeod, died in New Zealand on 16 June 1865. [F.4.87]

MCLEAN, NEIL, born 1788 on Rum, wife Mary born 1798, Margaret born 1812, and John, emigrated via Leith aboard the St Lawrence of Newcastle bound for Port Hawkesbury, Cape Breton, in 1828. [PANS.M6.100]

MACLEAN, NEIL, in Uisken, died in 1827, [Kilvickeon gravestone, Mull]

MCLEAN, NEIL, born 1800 on Rum, emigrated via Leith aboard the St Lawrence of Newcastle bound for Port Hawkesbury, Cape Breton, in 1828. [PANS.M6.100]

MCLEAN, NORMAN, with Peggy, and children John, Norman, and Margaret, from Skye aboard the Malay bound for Sydney, Nova Scotia, in 1830. [NSARM.RG1.67/19]

MCLEAN, NORMAN, born 1807, Marion born 1808, Peter born 1843, and Mary born 1845, emigrated via Liverpool aboard the Araminta bound for Australia on 20 June 1852. [NRS.HD4/5]

MCLEAN, NORMAN, born on Uist, on 11 October 1814, son of Reverend Duncan McLean and his wife Flora McLeod, died in Australia on 16 June 1865. [F.7.196]

MCLEAN, RONALD, Captain of the Rum Volunteer Infantry, a letter dated 8 October 1808. [NRS.GD23.6.449]

MCLEAN, SARAH, born 1782, a spinner from Mull, emigrated from Oban aboard the Clarendon of Hull, bound for Charlottetown, Prince Edward Island, in August 1808. [TNA.CO226.23]

MCLEAN, ..., his wife, four children, and two servants, from Mull, emigrated to Hudson Bay in 1812. [NAC.SP[C1] 294, 558-561]

MCLELLAN, ANGUS, from North Uist, married Sarah Philips from Halifax, New Brunswick, there on 2 September 1838. [Acadian Recorder, 8.9.1838]

MCLELLAN, ALEXANDER, born 1818 on Lewis, settled in Nova Scotia in 1830, died in July 1865. [Little Narrows Cemetery, Victoria County, Nova Scotia]

MCLELLAN, ANGUS, from North Uist, married Sarah Philips in Halifax, Nova Scotia, on 2 September 1838. [Acadian Recorder, 8 September 1838]

MCLELLAN, ARCHIBALD, emigrated from Uist to Nova Scotia in 1802, settled at Bailey Brook, Pictou County. [NSARM.RG20.Series A]

MCLELLAN, ARCHIBALD, ['son of Calum the fair', *mac Chalum bhan*], with his wife Marion MacLeod, and family, were evicted from Bun na Liggie, South Uist, and sent to America in the 1840s. [SCA.DA9.43]

MACLELLAN, DONALD, the fair, [*ban*], [son of Lachlan, son of Donald, son of John, son of John, *'mac Lachlan ic Dhomhnull ic Ian ic Ian'*], his wife Marcella Ferguson, and their family, were evicted from Oainish, South Uist, and sent to America in the 1840s. [SCA.DA9.43]

MCLELLAN, JOHN, born 1788, from Uig, Lewis, emigrated to the Red River settlement in 1811. [PAC.M155.145]

MCLELLAN, JOHN, a linen weaver in Keills, Islay, in 1828. [I.247]

MCLELLAN, WILLIAM, a linen weaver in Keills, Islay, in 1828. [I.247]

MCLENNAN, ALEXANDER, with his wife, two daughters and one infant, formerly in Raasay, later in Peiness, [Peighinn an Easa], Skye, applied to emigrate to Australia in 1854. [NRS.GD4437.1]

MCLENNAN, Mrs EFFY, born 1807, Angus born 1822, Catherine born 1829, Mary born 1831, Neil born 1833, Marion born 1839, John born 1841, and Donald born 1853, emigrated from Harris on board the Clansman bound for Australia on 13 July 1857. [NRS.GD371.241.1]

MCLENNAN, EWAN, born 1802 in Killilan, son of John McLennan and his wife Catherine McRae, a planter in Jamaica, died 1850 on Skye. [Kiel Duich gravestone]

MCLENNAN, KENNETH, born 1792, Christy born 1797, Norman born 1822, Christy born 1826, Mary born 1831, Catherine born

1833, Samuel born 1842, also Duncan born 1824 with Flora born 1824, and John born 1850, from Kilmaluag, Skye, emigrated via Liverpool aboard the Allison bound for Melbourne, Australia, on 13 September 1852. [NRS.HD4/5]

MCLENNAN, KENNETH, born 1827, Mary born 1833, emigrated from Harris on board the Clansman bound for Australia on 13 July 1857. [NRS.GD371.241.1]

MCLEOD, AGGRAPINA ZAGGREWSKI, daughter of Alexander N. MacLeod from Harris, married Jose Maria Magallon, at the Spanish Legation, Washington, USA, on 12 August 1852. [W.13.1362]

MCLEOD, ALEXANDER, of Ose, [Os], Bracadale, [Bracadal], Skye, died 18 June 1819, Edict of Executry, 20 March 1823. [NRS.CC12.7.47.1]

MCLEOD, ALEXANDER, an out-pensioner of the Chelsea Hospital, of the 6th Veteran Battalion, residing at Carabost, Bracadale, Skye, died there on 23 December 1816, husband of Mary Campbell, an edict of executry 25 May 1822. [NRS.CC12.7.46.6]

MCLEOD, ALEXANDER, born 1812, Mary born 1817, Donald born 1837, Norman born 1839, William born 1839, James born 1841, John born 1845, Roderick born 1848, and Hugh born 1851, from Culnacurrock, emigrated via Liverpool aboard the Araminta bound for Geelong, Australia, on 20 June 1852. [NRS.HD4/5]

MCLEOD, ALEXANDER NORMAN, of Harris, [Na Hearadh], 1832. [NRS.CS96.239]

MCLEOD, ALEXANDER, born in Kilfinichen, [Cill Fhionnchain], Mull, on 12 June 1774, son of Reverend Neil McLeod and his wife Margaret McLean, a minister of the Reformed

Presbyterian Church of New York, married Mary Ann Agnew on 16 September 1805. [F.4.113][M.33]

MCLEOD, ALEXANDER, son of Captain Norman McLeod [died 1804] and his wife Ann McLeod, [died 1830], died in the West Indies. [Dunvegan gravestone, Skye]

MCLEOD, ALEXANDER, on Raasay, emigrated to Prince Edstward Island in 1821. [SPI.162]

MCLEOD, ALEXANDER, in Ballione, Uist, victim of a crime in 1837. [NRS.AD14.37.35]

MACLEOD, ANGUS, born 1797 on Skye, son of Malcolm MacLeod and his wife Effie MacDonald, emigrated aboard the Polly in 1803 bound for Belfast, Prince Edward Island, died on 28 January 1885. [SP]

MCLEOD, ANGUS, born 1837 on Islay, settled in Caledon, Peel County, Ontario, died 25 October 1906. [Caledon gravestone]

MACLEOD, ANNE, born on Skye, daughter of Malcolm MacLeod and his wife Effie MacDonald, emigrated aboard the Polly in 1803 bound for Belfast, Prince Edward Island, married Alexander MacLeod from Skye. [SP]

MCLEOD, ANN, a widow, with one son and three daughters, from Colliemore, Skye, applied to emigrate to Australia in 1854. [NRS.GD221.4437.1]

MCLEOD, ARCHIBALD, son of Captain Norman McLeod [died 1804] tacksman of Bernisdale, [Bearnasdal], Skye, and his wife Ann [died 1830], settled in Marywate, New South Wales. [Dunvegan gravestone, Skye]

MCLEOD, CATHERINE, with her sister, from Camustinaveg, [Camustiannavaig], Skye, applied to emigrate to Australia in 1854. [NRS.GD221.4437.1]

MACLEOD, CHRISTINA, born on Skye, daughter of Malcolm MacLeod and his wife Effie MacDonald, emigrated aboard the Polly in 1803 bound for Belfast, Prince Edward Island, married Donald McQueen, died in Orwell, PEI in 1862. [SP]

MCLEOD, CHRISTY, with her two sons, from Colliemore, Skye, applied to emigrate to Australia in 1854. [NRS.GD221.4437.1]

MCLEOD, D., on Harris, a letter, 1804. [NRS.GD248.668.10]

MCLEOD, DONALD, tenant of Lord MacDonald in Kendram, Skye, bound for America around 1802. [NRS.GD221.4433.1]

MCLEOD, DONALD, tenant of Lord MacDonald in Maligar, Skye, bound for America around 1802. [NRS.GD221.4433.1]

MCLEOD, DONALD BAN OIG, from Valtos, [Bhaltos], Skye, with his wife Mary Martin, and children Donald, John, Malcolm, Roderick, Samuel, Nancy, Margaret, and Catherine, emigrated to Prince Edward Island in 1829. [SP.141]

MCLEOD, DONALD, born 1818 on Skye, son of Donald Ban Oig McLeod and his wife Mary Martin, settled in Uigg, Prince Edward Island in 1829, died in Middlesex, Ontario, in 1896. [SP]

MCLEOD, DONALD, son of Magnus McLeod and his wife Margaret Isabella MacDonald in Talisker, [Talaisker], Skye, emigrated from Skye aboard the Skelton bound for Van Diemen's Land, Australia, in 1820, settled in Sydney, New South Wales in 1837, died there on 11 April 1838. [TML.2.11]

MCLEOD, DONALD, with Mary and children John, Anne, Margaret, Donald, Malcolm, Roderick, Samuel, and Mary, from Skye aboard the Malay bound for Sydney, Nova Scotia, in 1830. [NSARM.RG1.67/19]

MCLEOD, DONALD, born 1818, Ann born 1822, Mary born 1841, Christy born 1844, Ann born 1847, and Malcolm born

1850, from Culnocnock, [Cul nan Cnoc], Skye, emigrated via Liverpool aboard the Ticonderoga bound for Port Philip, Australia, on 4 August 1852. [NRS.HD4/5]

MCLEOD, DONALD, born 1807, Flora born 1812, Angus born 1835, Norman born 1838, Alexander born 1839, Archibald born 1841, James born 1844, Neil born 1846, and Ewan born 1849, from Garasade, [An Garradh], Skye, emigrated via Liverpool aboard the Allison bound for Melbourne, Australia, on 13 September 1852. [NRS.HD4/5]

MCLEOD, DONALD, born 1822, Effy born 1822, Christy born 1845, Mary born 1848, Flora born 1850, and Kate born 1851, from Tormichaig, emigrated via Liverpool aboard the Priscilla bound for Victoria, Australia, on 15 October 1852. [NRS.HD4/5]

MCLEOD, DONALD, with his wife, and daughter, from Colliemore, Skye, applied to emigrate to Australia in 1854. [NRS.GD221.4437.1]

MCLEOD, DONALD, with his wife and three daughters, from Moorlands, Skye, emigrated to Australia on board the Arabian in 1854. [NRS.GD221.4437.1]

MCLEOD, DONALD, with his wife and daughter, from Uig, Skye, applied to emigrate to Australia in 1854. [NRS.GD221.4437.1]

MCLEOD, DOUGALD, born 1816, Mary born 1819, Peggy born 1841, Norman born 1843, Donald born 1845, and Malcolm born 1851, from Glen Skeabost, Skye, emigrated via Glasgow on board the Georgiana bound for Port Philip, Australia, on 13 July 1852. [NRS.HD4/5]

MCLEOD, DUGALD, with his wife, a son and four daughters, from Cuidrach, Skye, applied to emigrate to Australia in 1854. [NRS.GD221.4437.1]

MCLEOD, EURY, daughter of John McLeod in Ballinicoill, Uig, Lewis, accused of infanticide in 1815. [NRS.AD14.15.88]

MCLEOD, HECTOR, born 1802, Anne born 1811, Murdo born 1832, Effy born 1836, Alexander born 1843, and Mary, from Stein Seabost, Skye, emigrated via Liverpool aboard the Araminta bound for Geelong, Australia, on 20 June 1852. [NRS.HD4/5]

MCLEOD, HUGH NORMAN, born 30 November 1818 in Coll Castle, Isle of Coll, son of Donald McLeod and his wife Catherine MacLean, emigrated from Skye to Van Diemen's Land, Australia, aboard the Skelton in 1820, settled at Geelong, Victoria, died on 9 March 1892. [TML.2.12]

MCLEOD, ISABELLA, born 1800, wife of David Borrie gardener at Torloisk, died 26 July 1831. [Torloisk gravestone, Mull]

MCLEOD, JAMES, of Raasay, [Ratharsaigh], deceased, an inventory, 1825. [NRS.GD2.6.605]

MCLEOD, JANET, born in 1816, wife of Angus Steel at Loch Skippart, [Sgioport], South Uist, was accused of sheep stealing in 1849. [NRS.AD14.49.220]

MCLEOD, JOHN, a Loyalist, in Barraig, Skye, testament confirmed with the Commissariat of the Isles on 28 April 1797. [NRS]

MCLEOD, JOHN, born 1787 on Skye, emigrated to America in 1802, husband of Nancy McIver, died 24 October 1877, buried in Union Presbyterian cemetery, Moore County, North Carolina. [Moore County gravestone]

MCLEOD, JOHN, the younger, a labourer in Coilesdader, Portree, Skye, 1818. [NRS.AD14.18.89]

MCLEOD, JOHN, born on Skye before 1815, son of Norman McLeod and his wife Margaret MacPhee, emigrated to Prince Edward Island in 1829. [SP]

MCLEOD, JOHN, of Raasay, a debtor in 1834, 1846. [NRS.CS228.B17.103; GD1.1003.93.1846]

MCLEOD, JOHN, born 1807, Mary born 1817, Murdoch born 1846, Angus born 1848, and Malcolm born 1850, from Horneval, [Hornabhal], Skye, emigrated via Liverpool aboard the Allison bound for Melbourne, Australia, on 13 September 1852. [NRS.HD4/5]

MCLEOD, JOHN, born 1824, Catherine born 1832, from Monksleat, [Mogastad], Skye, emigrated via Liverpool aboard the Allison bound for Melbourne, Australia, on 13 September 1852. [NRS.HD4/5]

MCLEOD, JOHN, with a son, a daughter, one sister, and a male cousin, from Moorlands, Skye, emigrated to Australia on board the Arabian in 1854. [NRS.GD221.4437.1]

MCLEOD, JOHN, and his sister, from Mugarry, Skye, applied to emigrate to Australia in 1854. [NRS.GD221.4437.1]

MCLEOD, KATHERINE, youngest daughter of Alexander Norman McLeod from Harris, married M. de Bourboulon, the minister from France to China, in Baltimore on 28 April 1851. [W.1234]

MCLEOD, MAGNUS, born 30 November 1808 in Talisker, Skye, son of Donald McLeod and his wife Catherine MacLean, emigrated from Skye aboard the Skelton bound for Van Diemen's Land, Australia, in 1820, died there in 1886. [TML.2.17]

MCLEOD, MALCOLM, tenant of Lord MacDonald in Maligar, Skye, bound for America around 1802. [NRS.GD221.4433.1]

MCLEOD, MALCOLM, from Glashvin, Skye, emigrated aboard the Polly to Belfast, Prince Edward Island, in 1803. [SP]

MCLEOD, MALCOLM, born 1804, from North Uist, Marion born 1814, Margaret born 1833, John born 1835, Marion born 1837, Ann born 1841, Donald born 1843, and Angus born 1848, from North Uist, emigrated via Greenock aboard the Waterhen of London bound for Quebec in 1849. [NRS.GD221.4435]

MCLEOD, MALCOLM, born 1814, Euphemia born 1814, Katherine born 1837, Allan born 1839, Margaret born 1843, Janet born 1846, and Alexander born 1848, from North Uist, emigrated via Greenock aboard the Cashmere of Glasgow bound for Quebec in 1849. [NRS.GD221.4011.53]

MCLEOD, MALCOLM, born 1811, Sarah born 1809, Mary born 1839, Kenneth born 1841, Malcolm born 1845, and Janet born 1848, from Braebost on the Lyndale Estate, Skye, emigrated via Liverpool aboard the Araminta bound for Geelong, Australia, on 20 June 1852. [NRS.HD4/5]

MCLEOD, MARIAN, with three daughters, one nephew, and a male relative, from Fairfield, Skye, emigrated to Australia in 1854. [NRS.GD221.4437.1]

MCLEOD, MARY, with two sons and two daughters, from Camustinavaig, Skye, emigrated to Australia on board the Edward Johnstone in 1854. [NRS.GD221.4437.1]

MCLEOD, MURDOCH, in Portree, Skye, accused of theft, 6 April 1801. [NRS.AC26.1801.1]

MCLEOD, MURDO, with four brothers and two sisters, from Colliemore, Skye, applied to emigrate to Australia in 1854. [NRS.GD221.4437.1]

MCLEOD, MURDOCH, born 1784 on Harris, a veteran of the Battle of Trafalgar, emigrated to Prince Edward Island in 1816, died 23 May 1860, buried at Belfast, PEI. [SP]

MCLEOD, MURDOCH, born 1815 on Skye, son of Norman McLeod and his wife Margaret McPhee, emigrated to Prince Edward Island in 1829, married Margaret Gunn in Miramachi, Nova Scotia, on 6 October 1837, died on 29 July 1889. [SP.160]

MCLEOD, MURDOCH, in Mealista, [Mhealasta], Uig, was accused of the murder of Christian McLeod there in 1837. [NRS.AD37.27]

MCLEOD, MURDOCH, born 1812, Flora born 1815, John born 1840, Neil born 1846, and Catherine born 1850, from Conasda, [Conasta], Skye, emigrated via Liverpool aboard the Allison bound for Melbourne, Australia, on 13 September 1852. [NRS.HD4/5]

MCLEOD, NANCY MCIVER, born on Skye around 1787, emigrated to America in 1802, settled in North Carolina, died on 24 October 1877, buried in Union Cemetery, Carthage, Moore County, North Carolina. [Moore County gravestone]

MCLEOD, Captain NEIL, in Gesto, [Geusdo], Bracadale, Skye, a letter re the sale of property in the Bahama Islands by Lachlan McLeod the minister of St Kilda, dated 1812. [NRS.GD23.6.494]

MCLEOD, NORMAN, born on Skye, died in Montreal, Quebec, on 27 January 1796. [GM.66.614]

MCLEOD, NORMAN, born 1808, a blacksmith in Tarbert, Harris, [Tairbeart Na Hearadh], was accused of sheep stealing in 1836. [NRS.AD14.36.38]

MCLEOD, N., of McLeod, at Dunvegan, [Dun Mheagain], Skye, a letter, 1818. [NRS.GD201.6.49.6]

MCLEOD, PEGGY, born 1836, from Kilraxter, [Cille Bhacaister], Skye, emigrated via Liverpool aboard the Priscilla bound for Victoria, Australia, on 15 October 1852. [NRS.HD4/5]

MACLEOD, RODERICK, born 1777 on Barra, son of Gilleanan MacLeod, emigrated to Prince Edward Island in 1802, married Catharine Mac Eachern in 1811, parents of Roderick, Lauchlan, Donald, Margaret, Marjory, Catherine, Janet, and Ann, died 1850. [TML]

MCLEOD, RODERICK, with his wife and two sons from Inveralleveg, Skye, emigrated to Australia on board the Arabian in 1854. [NRS.GD221.4437.1]

MCLEOD, RODERICK, born 1825, Hanna born 1834, John born 1855, and Ann born 1856, emigrated from Harris on board the Clansman bound to Australia on 13 July 1857. [NRS.GD371.241.1]

MCLEOD, RODERICK, born 1812, Ann born 18, Mary Ann born 1843, John A. born 1845, and Jessie born 1847, emigrated from Harris on board the Clansman bound for Australia on 13 July 1857. [NRS.GD371.241.1]

MCLEOD, ROBERT, a fisherman on Tanera, a letter, 1836. [NRS.AF.1.38]

MCLEOD, RODERICK, born 1803 on Skye, son of Norman McLeod and his wife Margaret MacPhee, emigrated to Prince Edward Island in 1829, died 2 December 1882. [SP.160]

MCLEOD, RODRICK, and his wife Catherine McLeod, on Handa, [Eilean Shannda], were parents of Murdoch baptised there in 1828. [HS.20.5]

MCLEOD, Reverend R., in Skeabost, [Sgeubost], Skye, a letter to Lord McDonald's factor concerning the eviction of tenants in 1846. [NRS.GD45.13], died 2 December 1882. [SP.160]

MCLEOD, RORY, tenant of Lord MacDonald in Kendram, Skye, bound for America around 1802. [NRS.GD221.4433.1]

MCLEOD, SAMUEL, born 1796 on Skye, son of Norman McLeod and his wife Margaret MacPhee, emigrated to Prince Edward Island in 1829, husband of Margaret Currie, a Baptist minister in Uigg and Belfast, P.E.I., from 1840-1870, died 23 August 1881. [SP.159]

MCLEOD, SARAH, born 1809, wife of Archibald McLellan in Clachan, Loch Carron, South Uist, was accused of sheep stealing in 1849. [NRS.AD14.49.220]

MCLEOD, SARRY, born 1780 on Sleat, died in North Carolina in September 1812, buried in Union Cemetery, Carthage, Moore County, North Carolina. [Moore County gravestone]

MCLEOD, TORQUIL, born 1828, Margaret born 1825, Christy born 1824, Alexander born 1837, Ann born 1828, Neil born 1841, Catherine born 1845, and Catherine born 1848, from Raasay, emigrated via Liverpool on board the Ticonderoga bound for Port Philip, Australia, on 4 August 1852. [NRS.HD4/5]

MACLEOD, WILLIAM, born 1770 on Skye, son of William MacLeod of Millivaig, [Miolabhaig], Skye, emigrated to North Carolina aboard the Duke of Kent in 1802, settled in Moore County, died 25 January 1864, buried at Bethesda, North Carolina. [TML]

MCLEOD, WILLIAM, born 1795 on Lewis, died 10 April 1874, husband of Isabella, born 1798 on Lewis, died 2 February 1874. [Little Narrows Cemetery, Victoria County, Nova Scotia]

MCLEOD, WILLIAM, late of Luskintyre, [Losgaintir], Harris, tacksman of Borlett, 1811, he died in Bracadale, Skye. [NRS.CC12.74.41.7]

MCLEOD, WILLIAM, born 1802, Malcolm born 1836, Mary born 1830, Isabella born 1832, and Janet born 1838, from Glenhamerdale, emigrated via Liverpool aboard the Allison bound for Melbourne, Australia, on 13 September 1852. [NRS.HD4/5]

MCLEOD, WILLIAM, tenant of Ardellum, Ulva, in 1824. [NRS.GD174.1140.9]

MCLEOD, Mrs, a widow, with three sons and two daughters, from Balmeanoch, Skye, applied to emigrate to Australia in 1854. [NRS.GD221.4437.1]

MACLUGASH, DONALD, in Esknish, [Easganais], Islay, 1818.[NRS.GD64.1.112]

MCLIESH, JOHN, minister at Kilchoman, Islay, in 1794. [I.188]

MCLUISH, DONALD, born 1785, with Mary born 1807, Ann born1830, Neil born1832, and Flora born 1834, from North Uist, emigrated via Greenock aboard the Waterhen of London bound for Quebec in 1849. [NRS.GD221.4435]

MCLUISH, JOHN, born 1798, Kate born 1822, Donald born 1836, Ewan born 1838, Murdo born 1840, Mary born 1842, Donald junior born 1844, Christy born 1847, from North Uist, emigrated via Greenock aboard the Cashmere of Glasgow bound for Quebec in 1849. [NRS.GD221.4011.53]

MCLUISH, NORMAN, born 1802, Catherine born 1817, Marion born 1834, Donald born 1843, Angus born 1845, Margaret born 1847, and Archie born 1848, from North Uist, emigrated via Greenock aboard the Cashmere of Glasgow bound for Quebec in 1849. [NRS.GD221.4011.53]

MCMAY, NEIL, born 1826, with Kate born 1830, from North Uist, emigrated via Greenock aboard the Waterhen of London bound for Quebec in 1849. [NRS.GD221.4435]

MCMILLAN, alias MCILLIVAOIL, ALEXANDER, from Canna, [Canaigh], a shopbreaker, was sentenced to be transported for 14 years, at Inveraray on 13 September 1811. [SM.83.10/790]

MCMILLAN, ANGUS, from Mull, emigrated aboard the Commerce via Tobermory to Port Hastings, in 1822, settled at East Lake, Nova Scotia.

MCMILLAN, ANGUS, born 1790 on Rum, emigrated via Leith aboard the St Lawrence of Newcastle bound for Port Hawkesbury, Cape Breton, in 1828. [PANS.M6.100]

MCMILLAN, ANN, born 1800 on Rum, emigrated via Leith aboard the St Lawrence of Newcastle bound for Port Hawkesbury, Cape Breton, in 1828. [PANS.M6.100]

MCMILLAN, ARCHIBALD, born 1801 on Rum, wife Jessie born 1800, Donald born 1826, Neil an infant, emigrated via Leith aboard the St Lawrence of Newcastle bound for Port Hawkesbury, Cape Breton, in 1828. [PANS.M6.100]

MCMILLAN, CATHERINE, from Mull, emigrated aboard the Commerce via Tobermory, Mull, to Port Hastings, Nova Scotia, in 1822, settled at East Lake, Nova Scotia.

MCMILLAN, CHRISTINA, born 1768 on Rum, emigrated via Leith aboard the St Lawrence of Newcastle bound for Port Hawkesbury, Cape Breton, in 1828. [PANS.M6.100]

MCMILLAN, DONALD, from Mull, emigrated aboard the Commerce via Tobermory to Port Hastings, Nova Scotia, in 1822, settled at East Lake, Nova Scotia.

MCMILLAN, DONALD, born 1771 on Rum, wife Marion born 1786, emigrated via Leith aboard the St Lawrence of Newcastle bound for Port Hawkesbury, Cape Breton, in 1828. [PANS.M6.100]

MCMILLAN, DUNCAN, from Mull, emigrated aboard the Commerce via Tobermory to Port Hastings, in 1822, settled at East Lake, Nova Scotia.

MCMILLAN, DUNCAN, in Ardelamy, Gigha, 1841. [NRS.SC50.841.59]

MCMILLAN, DUNCAN, in Ardachy, [Ardachaidh], Gigha, 1841. [NRS.SC50.5.1841.60]

MACMILLAN, DUNCAN, cottar at Iculs Glen, Gigha, in 1849. [NRS.SC50.5.1849.3]

MCMILLAN, DUNCAN, a cottar in Glen Ardminish, Gigha, 1848. [NRS.SC50.5.1848.32]

MCMILLAN, ISABEL, born 1788 on Islay, died in North Carolina on 1 July 1850, buried in Phillips cemetery, Raeford, Hoke County, N.C. [Hoke gravestone]

MCMILLAN, JAMES, born 1783 on Colonsay, [Colbhasa], emigrated to Prince Edward Island in 1806, died there on 11 February 1861, his wife Ann Munn, born 1788 on Colonsay, died on P.E.I. on 10 March 1870. [Woods Island Pioneer Cemetery, P.E.I.]

MCMILLAN, JOHN, born 1761 on Rum, with Catherine born 1802, Mary born 1804, Ann born 1805, Flora born 1811, and Neil born 1815, emigrated via Leith aboard the St Lawrence of Newcastle bound for Port Hawkesbury, Cape Breton, in 1828. [PANS.M6.100]

MCMILLAN, JOHN, and family, from South Uist, settled in Orangedale, Cape Breton, in 1840.

MCMILLAN, MALCOLM, from Mull, emigrated aboard the Commerce via Tobermory to Port Hastings, N.S., in 1822, settled at East Lake, Nova Scotia.

MCMILLAN, MARIAN, born 1788 on Rum, emigrated via Leith aboard the St Lawrence of Newcastle bound for Port Hawkesbury, Cape Breton, in 1828. [PANS.M6.100]

MCMILLAN, MARIAN, born 1811 on Rum, emigrated via Leith aboard the St Lawrence of Newcastle bound for Port Hawkesbury, Cape Breton, in 1828. [PANS.M6.100]

MCMILLAN, NEIL, born 1804 on Rum, emigrated via Leith aboard the St Lawrence of Newcastle bound for Port Hawkesbury, Cape Breton, in 1828. [PANS.M6.100]

MCMILLAN, NEIL, from Mull, emigrated aboard the Commerce via Tobermory to Port Hastings, N.S., in 1822, settled at East Lake, Nova Scotia.

MCMILLAN, PETER, from South Uist, emigrated to Nova Scotia, settled at River Dennis.

MCMILLAN, RORY, a blacksmith from South Uist, emigrated to Nova Scotia, settled at Port Hood, Nova Scotia.

MCMORRAN, ARCHIBALD, was accused of sheep stealing on Staffa in 1831. [NRS.AD14.31.195]

MACMULLIN, RUAIRAIDH, born 1795, with his wife Caitriona MacNeil, from Bruernish, Barra, possibly emigrated on board the Harmony to Cape Breton in 1821.

MCNABB, DUNCAN, born 1798 on Islay, emigrated via Greenock to Charleston, South Carolina, naturalised on 11 March 1830 in Marlborough County, S.C. [SCSA]

MCNAB, JOHN, born 1792, from Islay, emigrated via Glasgow on board the Damuscus bound for Toronto, Canada, on 28 June 1862. [JRK]

MCNAB, JOHN, born 1835, John born 1859, and Peter born 1861, from Islay, emigrated via Glasgow on board the Damuscus bound for Toronto, Canada, on 28 June 1862. [JRK]

MCNAB, JOHN, with Kate and children Mary, Anne, Andrew, John, and Marion, from Skye aboard the Malay bound for Sydney, Nova Scotia, in 1830. [NSARM.RG1.67/19]

MCNAIR, DONALD, born 1756, Marrin McGilvray born 1768, Roderick born 1786, Donald born 1788, Ann born 1790, Flora born 1792, Marren born 1797, from Tobermory, Mull, aboard the brig Isle of Skye bound for Prince Edward Island in 1806. [PAPEI.2702]

MCNAUGHTON, NEIL, born 1805, a fisherman in Bowmore, Islay, was accused of theft from Neill Ferguson of Claddoch Farm, Kilchoman, Islay, in 1829. [NRS.AD14.29.316]

MCNEILL, Captain ALEXANDER, eldest son of John McNeill of Colonsay, a sasine 1834. [NRS.GD64.3.4]

MCNEILL, ALEXANDER, of Gigha, 1839, 1841, 1849. [NRS.SC50.1839.18; 1841.59/60]

MCNEIL, ANNE, at Castlebay, Barra, accused of theft in 1842. [NRS.AD14.42.151]

MCNEIL, ARCHIBALD, from Colonsay, HM Consul for Louisiana, died on his way from Canada to New York in 1808. [EA.4607]; 1809. [NRS.CS17.1.29/104]

MCNEILL, Colonel ARCHIBALD, of Colonsay, letters 1805-1808. [NRS.GD1.431.15; GD64.1.169]; probate, 28 January 1809, Prerogative Court of Canterbury. [TNA]

MCNEILL, CHARLES, from Demerara, son of Captain Alexander McNeill of Colonsay, married Margaret McNeill, only child of Malcolm McNeill of Lossit, on 5 November 1840 in Glasgow. [W.88]

MCNEILL, DONALD, born 1789, died 16 March 1879. [Kilviceuen gravestone, Ulva]

MCNEILL, DONALD, in Canna, a letter dated 14 February 1804. [NRS.NRAS.2177.1522]

MCNEIL, DONALD, from Uist, settled at the Mira River, Cape Breton, in 1847. [NRS.GD403.27]

MCNEIL, DONALD JOHN, from Uist, a merchant in Sydney, Nova Scotia, in 1848. [NRS.GD403.27]

MCNEIL, DONALD, born 1826 on Barra, died 26 March 1885 on Cape Breton. [St Andrew's RC Cemetery, Boisdale, Cape Breton]

MCNEIL, GRACE, born 1762 on Colonsay, wife of Malcolm McMillan, died on Prince Edward Island on 3 January 1833. [Woods Island Pioneer Cemetery]

MCNEIL, HECTOR, son of Hector Og McNeil of Orsary, Barra, emigrated to Pictou, Nova Scotia, in 1802. [CMN]

MCNEILL, HECTOR, of Canna, a letter regarding the inhabitants of Sanday Island, dated 2 June 1802. [NRS.NRAS.2177.1512]

MCNEIL, HUGH, born 1787 in Mull, a labourer, emigrated from Oban aboard the Clarendon of Hull, bound for Charlottetown, Prince Edward Island, in August 1808. [TNA.CO226.23]

MCNEILL, ISABELLA, born 1841 in Tobermory, Mull, emigrated via Liverpool aboard the Panama bound for Van Dieman's Land Australia, in 1853. [NRS.HD4/5]

MCNEILL, JAMES, born 1794 on Barra, died 9 September 1878. [St Andrew's RC Cemetery, Boisdale, Cape Breton]

MCNEIL, or MORRISON, JANET, re Gigha in 1836. [NRS.CS230.MC.10/21]

MCNEILL, JOHN, from Barra, settled at Grand Narrows, Cape Breton in 1804. [CMN]

MCNEIL, JOHN, born 1779, a cooper from Killocran, Colonsay, with his children Catherine born 1814, Archibald born 1817, and Laughlan born 1820, were due to emigrate via Liverpool aboard the Ayrshire of Liverpool bound for Quebec in 1844, to settle on Prince Edward Island. [NRS.CS235/S47.11]

MCNEIL, JOHN, born 1791, a labourer from Mull, emigrated from Oban aboard the Clarendon of Hull, bound for Charlottetown, Prince Edward Island, in August 1808. [TNA.CO226.23]

MCNEILL, JOHN, of Gigha, 1813. [NRS.CC2.7.61/5]

MCNEILL, JOHN, the younger of Gigha, a bond of caution, 19 July 1808. [NRS.CC2.9.6.8]

MCNEILL, JOHN, emigrated from Barra to Cape Breton in 1817. [CMN]

MCNEILL, JOHN, of Oakfield and Gigha, 22 August 1826. [NRS.GD43.30.177]

MACNEIL, JOHN, born 1817 on Barra, emigrated to Canada in 1823, died in Gillis, Prince Edward Island, husband of Katherine born on Iona in 1832, died 1881. [Iona gravestone, N.S.]

MCNEILL, JOHN, a tenant of Cradaig, Ulva, in 1824. [NRS.GD174.1087.1]

MCNEILL, JOHN, born 1825, from Tobermory, Mull, emigrated via Liverpool on the Panama bound for Van Diemen's Land, Australia, on 8 January 1853. [NRS.HD4/5]

MCNEIL, LACHLAN, born 1764, a former soldier of the 42nd [Black Watch] Regiment who had fought the French at Aboukir, died 23 December 1827. [Kilvickeon gravestone, Mull]

MCNEILL, LACHLAN, born 1833, from Tobermory, Mull, emigrated via Liverpool on the Panama bound for Van Diemen's Land, Australia, on 8 January 1853. [NRS.HD4/5]

MCNEILL, MALCOLM, on Oronsay, a letter, 31 December 1800. [NRS.GD1.431.14]

MCNEILL, MALCOLM, a merchant in Stornaway, Lewis, an edict of executry date 1810. [NRS.CC12.17.40.11]

MCNEILL, MALCOLM, in Lossit, Kilmany parish, Islay, 1838.

MCNEIL, MARGARET, daughter of Malcolm McNeil of Ardelister, married James McNab from Jamaica, on Islay on 27 February 1804. [CM.13029]

MCNEIL, MARY, from Uist, wife of Dr Jeans, on Cape Breton by 1848. [NRS.GD403.27]

MCNEIL, NEIL, born 1770, a labourer from Mull, wife Ann born 1770, and children Torquil born 1795, John born 1800, Duncan born 1802, Mary born 1798, and Catherine born 1804, emigrated from Oban aboard the Clarendon of Hull, bound for Charlottetown, Prince Edward Island, in August 1808. [TNA.CO226.23]

MCNEIL, NEIL, born 1770 on Jura, emigrated to North Carolina in 1792, settled in Cumberland County and later in Robeson County, died 1 June 1858. [St Paul's Register] [NCSA.WBC.384.7]

MCNEILL, NEILL, born 1784 on Jura, husband of Sarah ..... [1784-1860}, died in North Carolina on 17 September 1857, buried in Phillips cemetery, Raeford, Hoke County, N.C. [Hoke gravestone]

MCNIEL, NIEL, tenant of Aboss, Ulva, in 1824. [NRS.GD174.1140.9]

MCNIEL, NORMAND, on Babbay, Harris, a decreet, 1819. [NRS.CS40.31.58]

MCNEIL, RODERICK, born 1793 on Barra, died on 6 November 1856 on Cape Breton Island, Jane, his wife, born 1796 on Barra, died on 12 November 1867 on Cape Breton Island. [St Andrew's RC Cemetery, Boisdale, Cape Breton]

MCNEIL, R., on St Kilda, a letter ca.1802. [NRS.GD9.159]

MCNEIL, RODERICK, of Barra, a letter dated 28 January 1804. [NRS.NRAS.2177.1522]

MCNEIL, RODERICK, born in Barra in 1802, a carpenter, died in 1882. [St Andrew's RC Cemetery, Cape Breton, gravestone]

MCNEIL, RODERICK, born on Barra, [Eileen Bharraigh], in 1821, died on Long Island, Cape Breton, on 1 October 1910. [St Andrew's RC Cemetery, Cape Breton, gravestone]

MCNEILL, Mrs SALLY, born 1796 on Jura, wife of Neill McNeill, settled in Cumberland County, North Carolina, in 1820, died on 25 November 1860. [NCPresbyterian. 8.12.1860]

MCNIEL, WILLIAM, tacksman of St Kilda, a decreet, 1819. [NRS.CS40.31.58]

MCNEILL of Colonsay, papers, 1776-1844. [NRS.GD1.431]

MCNICOL, DONALD, minister of Jura and Colonsay, petitions, 1803. [NRS.GD64.1.174-175]; born 1735, died 28 March 1802, husband of Lillias Campbell, born 1759, died 30 June 1831. [Lismore gravestone]

MCNIVEN, ARCHIBALD, in Islay, claimed to have organised the emigration of 12,000 Highlanders to Cape Breton, Nova Scotia, Prince Edward Island, and Upper Canada between 1821 and 1832.

MACNIVEN, JANE, born 1806, married John MacDonald in North Uist, emigrated to Canada in 1822. [SG.33.2.199]

MCNIVEN, JULIA, born 1805 on Tiree, died 11 June 1843, wife of John Noble a surgeon. [Stewartdale Cemetery, Inverness County, Nova Scotia]

MACOUARTE, LACHLAN, born 1779, late a Captain of the 86th [Royal County Down] Regiment of Foot, died 6 July 1821, husband of Mary Shaw. [Kilpatrick gravestone, Mull]

MCPHADEN, HECTOR, wife Ann, children Donald, John and Angus, from Rum, emigrated via Leith aboard the St Lawrence of Newcastle bound for Port Hawkesbury, Cape Breton, in 1828. [PANS.M6.100]

MCPHAIL, ANGUS, born 1818, died 14 May 1882, husband of
[1] Mary Campbell at Achnacraig, born 1816, died 17 August
1849, [2] Catherine McLachlan, born 1826, died 14 March
1912. [Kilpatrick Duart gravestone, Torosay]

MCPHAIL, ARCHIBALD, born 1823, Christian born 1824, and
Christian born 1848, from North Uist, emigrated via Greenock
aboard the Waterhen of London bound for Quebec in 1849.
[NRS.GD221.4435]

MACPHAIL, DONALD, born 1789, tenant in Ardun, died 1 April
1855, husband of Isabella Rose, born 1787, died 28 November
1831. [Kilvickeon gravestone, Mull]

MCPHAIL, DUGALD, born 1818, son of Donald McPhail [1779-
1832] and his wife Catherine Campbell [1786-1864], was
apprenticed to Neil Fletcher, a joiner at Penalbanach near
Tobermory, later returned to Torasay as miller and joiner
there, he died in 1887. [M.399/405]

MCPHAIL, HUGH, born 1823, wife Janet born 1830, with
brother Colin McPhail, from Iona, emigrated aboard the
Marmion in 1852 bound for Moreton Bay, Australia.
[NRS.HD4/5]

MCPHAIL, JOHN, born 1759, tennt in Ardtun, died 18 February
1817. [Kilpatrick gravestone, Mull]

MCPHAIL, JOHN, born 1836, from Islay, emigrated via Glasgow
on board the Damascus bound for Toronto, Canada, on 28 June
1862. [JRK]

MCPHAIL, MALCOLM, born 1770 on Jura, died in North
Carolina on 1 June 1851. [Longstreet gravestone, N.C.]

MCPHAIL, NEIL, a merchant in Tobermory, Mull, in 1843.
[M.274]

MCPHARDON, ALEXANDER, born 1778, Elizabeth born 1782, Angus born 1804, from Tobermory, Mull, aboard the brig Humphreys bound for Prince Edward Island in 1806. [PAPEI.2702]

MCPHEE, ANGUS, born 1818, Effy born 1818, John born 1839, Mary born 1842, and Christy born 1850, from Sighigan, emigrated via Liverpool aboard the Priscilla bound for Victoria, Australia, on 15 October 1852. [NRS.HD4/5]

MCPHEE, ARCHIBALD, born 1822, Anne born 1817, Anne born 1844, Catherine born 1848, and William born 1850, from Feull, emigrated via Liverpool aboard the Araminta bound for Geelong, Australia, on 20 June 1852. [NRS.HD4/5]

MCPHEE, ARCHIBALD, born 1816, Christy born 1816, Christy born 1839, Mary born 1842, Norman born 1844, and Jane born 1848, from Rhuenduennan, emigrated via Liverpool aboard the Priscilla bound for Victoria, Australia, on 15 October 1852. [NRS.HD4/5]

MCPHEE, DONALD, born 1816, Marion born 1816, Angus born 1839, Marion born 1840, Margaret born 1844, Norman born 1846, Mary born 1849, and Neil an infant, from Carbost, Skye, emigrated via Liverpool aboard the Priscilla bound for Victoria, Australia, on 15 October 1852. [NRS.HD4/5]

MCPHEE, JOHN, tenant of Ardellum, Ulva, in 1824. [NRS.GD174.1140.9]

MACPHEE, JOHN, his wife Marion MacDonald, and family, were evicted from Bun na Liggie, South Uist, and sent to America in the 1840s. [SCA.DA9.43]

MCPHEE, MARGARET, born 1792, Christy born 1823, and Alexander born 1826, from Rhuenduennan, emigrated via Liverpool aboard the Priscilla bound for Victoria, Australia, on 15 October 1852. [NRS.HD4/5]

MCPHERSON, ALEXANDER, late deputy barrack master at Duart Castle, Mull, an edict of executry, 1804. [NRS.CC12.7.36.6]

MCPHERSON, ANGUS, and his wife, from Renetra, Skye, emigrated to Australia on board the Arabian in 1854. [NRS.GD221.4437.1]

MCPHERSON, ANN, born 1823, Janet, born 1825, and Angus born 1832, from Kilmuir, [Cille Mhoire], Skye, emigrated via Liverpool aboard the Allison bound for Melbourne, Australia, on 13 September 1852. [NRS.HD4/5]

MCPHERSON, ARCHIBALD, tenant of Laggan, Ulva, 1824. [NRS.GD174.1140.9]

MCPHERSON, DONALD, with Marion and children Donald, John, Alexander, Mary, and Margaret, from Skye aboard the Malay bound for Sydney, Nova Scotia, in 1830. [NSARM.RG1.67/19]

MCPHERSON, DONALD, born 1781, cooper in Aros, died 18 November 1853, his wife Catherine McPhail, born 1779, died 3 February 1853. [Glen Aros gravestone, Mull]

MCPHERSON,DONALD, born 1796, from North Uist, Catherine born 1828, Flora born 1831, Donald born 1836, Lauchlan born 1838, and Angus born 1840, from North Uist, emigrated via Greenock aboard the Waterhen of London bound for Quebec in 1849. [NRS.GD221.4435]

MCPHERSON, DONALD, born 1817, Ann born 1822, and Donald born 1849, from Granalin, [Grealinn], Skye, emigrated via Liverpool aboard the Priscilla bound for Victoria, Australia, on 15 October 1852. [NRS.HD4/5]

MCPHERSON, DONALD, born 1824, Ann born 1823, Margaret born 1847, and Neil an infant, from Kilraxter, [Cille Bhacastair],

Skye, emigrated via Liverpool aboard the Priscilla bound for Victoria, Australia, on 15 October 1852. [NRS.HD4/5]

MCPHERSON, DONALD, with his wife, two sisters and two cousins, from Ollach, Skye, applied to emigrate to Australia in 1854. [NRS.GD221.4437.1]

MCPHERSON, DONALD, and his wife, from Uig, Skye, applied to emigrate to Australia in 1854. [NRS.GD221.4437.1]

MCPHERSON, EFFY, from Ollach, Skye, emigrated to Australia on the Arabian in 1854. [NRS.GD221.4437.1]

MCPHERSON, GELLIN, born 1768, Flora born 1773, Archibald born 1797, Mary born 1802, Margaret born 1804, from Tobermory, Mull, aboard the brig Humphreys bound for Prince Edward Island in 1806. [PAPEI.2702]

MCPHERSON, HANNAH, with one son and one daughter, from Portree, Skye, emigrated to Australia in 1854. [NRS.GD221.4437.1]

MACPHERSON, IAIN, with his wife Margaret, also his brother Aonghus MacPherson with his wife Mor MacIntyre and children Donald and Sarah, from Barra, possibly emigrated on board the Harmony to Cape Breton in 1821.

MCPHERSON, JOHN C., born 1787 in Mull, died in St John, New Brunswick, on 15 December 1829. [New Brunswick Courier, 19.12.1829]

MCPHERSON, JOHN, in Ardelamy, Gigha, 1841. [NRS.SC50.841.59]

MCPHERSON, MARY, born 1828, from Horneval, [Hornabhal], Skye, emigrated via Liverpool aboard the Allison bound for Melbourne, Australia, on 13 September 1852. [NRS.HD4/5]

MCPHERSON, MARY, from Peinmore, [Am Peighinn Mor], Skye, applied to emigrate to Australia in 1854. [NRS.GD221.4437.1]

MACPHERSON, MARY, born in March 1821, *Mairi Mhor nan Oran*, daughter of John MacDonald and his wife Flora Macinnes in Skeabost, Skye, married Isaac MacPherson a shoemaker, died in Portree, Skye, in 1898.

MCPHERSON, NEIL, born 1799, Katie born 1814, Archie born 1833, John born 1835, Margaret born 1839, James born 1842, Flora born 1844, Alexander born 1846, from North Uist, emigrated via Greenock aboard the Cashmere of Glasgow bound for Quebec in 1849. [NRS.GD221.4011.53]

MCPHERSON, PEGGY, born 1812, Fanny born 1832, John born 1836, Catherine born 1838, Christy born 1841, and William born 1843, from Portree, Mull, emigrated via Liverpool aboard the Priscilla bound for Victoria, Australia, on 15 October 1852. [NRS.HD4/5]

MACQUARRIE, ALLAN, a builder in Cragaig, husband of Marion Macarthur, born 1773, died 28 September 1828, parents of Lachlan, born 1809, died 16 May 1836, [Kilvickeuen gravestone, Ulva]

MCQUARRIE, ALLAN, born 1804, Catherine born 1813, Flora born 1844, Lachlan born 1845, and Hugh born 1848, from Tobermory, Mull, emigrated via Liverpool aboard the Panama bound for Van Diemen's Land, Australia, on 8 January 1853. [NRS.HD.4/5]

MCQUARIE, CATHERINE, born 1820, daughter of Archibald McQuarie a schoolmaster, died in August 1822. [Kilmore Dervaig gravestone, Mull]

MCQUARRIE, CHARLES, born 1806, son of Lachlan McQuarrie [1779-1821] and his wife Mary Shaw, was a leader of the Baptists in the Ross of Mull, a merchant in Bnessan, Mull, a member of the parochial board and inspector for Ross and Iona, died 1861. [M.351/358]

MCQUARRIE, Lieutenant Colonel CHARLES, of Ulva and Glenforsa, a trust disposition, 1850. [NRS.GD174.33]; Lieutenant Colonel of the 42nd [Black Watch] Regiment, husband of Mariann Willison, born 1792, died 3 September 1828. [Kilviceuen gravestone, Ulva]

MCQUARIE, DONALD, tenant of Aboss, Ulva, in 1824. [NRS.GD174.1140.9]

MCQUARRIE, FLORA, of Ulva, alias Mrs McLean of Kilbrennan, died in 1836. [M.182]

MCQUARIE, GUARIE, tenant of Ferinardry, Ulva, in 1824. [NRS.GD174.1140.9]

MCQUARRIE, HECTOR, born 1785, a labourer from Mull, emigrated from Oban aboard the Clarendon of Hull, bound for Charlottetown, Prince Edward Island, in August 1808. [TNA.CO226.23]

MCQUARRIE, HECTOR, tenant of Ferinardry, Ulva, in 1824. [NRS.GD174.1140.9]

MCQUARRIE, HECTOR, born 1808, a boatbuilder and a crofter, Mary born 1818, Christy born 1840, Hugh born 1843, Kate born 1845, and Donald born 1850, from Tobermory, Mull, emigrated via Liverpool aboard the Panama bound for Van Diemen's Land, Australia, on 8 January 1853. [NRS.HD.4/5]

MCQUARRIE, JOHN, born 1763 on Rum, wife Marion born 1768, Allan born 1798, Donald born 1800, Rachel born 1802, Margaret born 1804, Bell born 1808, emigrated via Leith aboard the St Lawrence of Newcastle bound for Port Hawkesbury, Cape Breton, in 1828. [PANS.M6.100]

MACQUARIE, JOHN, a tenant of Cragaig, Ulva, in 1824. [NRS.GD174.1087.1]

MCQUARRIE, JOHN, born 1816, Ann born 1810, from Tyree, [Tiriodh], emigrated via Liverpool aboard the Marmion bound for Moreton Bay, Australia, on 28 August 1852. [NRS.HD4/5]

MCQUARRIE, LACHLAN, on Colonsay, [Colbhasa], letters, 1788 – 1804. [NRS.GD174.1427][M.95]; deceased, a decreet, 1813. [NRS.CS40.14.1]

MACQUARRIE, of Jarvisfield, Major General LACHLAN, born 31 January 1761. Governor of New South Wales, Australia, in 1809, died in London 1 July 1824, husband of Elizabeth Henrietta Campbell, died 17 March 1835. [MacQuarrie Mausoleum, Mull]

MCQUARRIE, LACHLAN, born 1787, a labourer from Mull, emigrated from Oban aboard the Clarendon of Hull, bound for Charlottetown, Prince Edward Island, in August 1808. [TNA.CO226.23]

MCQUARRIE, LACHLAN, tenant of Glaknagallon, Ulva, in 1824. [NRS.GD174.1140.9]

MACQUARRIE, LACHLAN, born 1816, died in Salen on 24 December 1900, husband of Hannah Black, born 1825, died 2 March 1880. [Kilvickeuen gravestone, Ulva]

MCQUARRIE, MALCOLM, tenant of Aboss, Ulva, in 1824. [NRS.GD174.1140.9]

MCQUARRIE, MARGARET, born 1748, a spinner from Mull, emigrated from Oban aboard the Clarendon of Hull, bound for Charlottetown, Prince Edward Island, in August 1808. [TNA.CO226.23]

MACQUARIE, NIEL, tenant of Salen Ruadh, Ulva, in 1824. [NRS.GD174.1140.9]

MCQUARRIE, the widow, tenant of Glaknagallon, Ulva, in 1824. [NRS.GD174.1140.9]

MCQUEARY, ALEXANDER, born 1766, Isobel born 1773, Flora born 1793, Sarah born 1795, John born 1798, Sandy born 1800, Margaret born 1802, and Una born 1806, from Tobermory, Mull, aboard the brig Humphreys bound for Prince Edward Island in 1806. [PAPEI.2702]

MCQUEEN, ALEXANDER, with his wife, five sons, and one daughter, from Achinhanaig, Skye, applied to emigrate to Australia in 1854. [NRS.GD221.4437.1]

MCQUEEN, ANGUS, born 27 May 1764 on Skye, died in North Carolina on 27 January 1848, buried in Stewartsville cemetery, Laurinburg, Scotland County, N.C. [Laurinburg gravestone]

MCQUEEN, DANIEL, born 3 January 1794 on Barra, son of Reverend Edmond McQueen and his wife Mary McLean, a surgeon, died in Jamaica in 1819. [EEC.16854][F.7.186]

MCQUEEN, DONALD, born 1782 on Skye, emigrated to America in 1800, settled in Robeson County, North Carolina, died 23 July 1867 in Marion District, South Carolina. [NCPresbyterian, 28.8.1867]

MCQUEEN, Colonel DONALD, born 1783 on Skye, emigrated to America in 1802, died 23 July 1867, buried in Stewartsville cemetery, Laurinburg, Scotland County, North Carolina. [Laurenburg gravestone]

MCQUEEN, DONALD, with his wife, three sons and two daughters, from Coilliemore, Skye, applied to emigrate to Australia in 1854. [NRS.GD221.4437.1]

MCQUEEN, DONALD, with his wife, daughter, and sister, from Achnahanaig, Skye, applied to emigrate to Australia in 1854. [NRS.GD221.4437.1]

MCQUEEN, DONALD, with his wife, from Coilliemore, Skye, applied to emigrate to Australia in 1854. [NRS.GD221.4437.1]

MCQUEEN, EDMOND, in Barra, [Barraigh], a letter dated 2 February 1804. [NRS.NRAS.2177.1522]

MCQUEEN, EWEN, with his wife, four sons, two daughters, and an infant, from Camustinaveg, Skye, applied to emigrate to Australia in 1854. [NRS.GD221.4437.1]

MCQUEEN, FINLAY, born 1794, Christy born 1802, Malcolm born 1828, Rachel born 1833, and John born 1839, from St Kilda, emigrated via Liverpool aboard the Priscilla bound for Victoria, Australia, on 15 October 1852. [NRS.HD4/5]

MCQUEEN, FINLAY, the younger, born 1808, Catherine born 1808, Donald born 1834, Neil born 1845, Finlay born 1848, and Mary born 1851, from St Kilda, emigrated via Liverpool aboard the Priscilla bound for Victoria, Australia, on 15 October 1852. [NRS.HD4/5]

MCQUEEN, JANET, wife of Roderick McLeod the minister of Braccadale, Skye, an edict of executry, 1817. [NRS.CC12.7.44.4]

MCQUEEN, JOHN, with his wife, an infant, one brother, and two sisters, from Portree, Skye, applied to emigrate to Australia in 1854. [NRS.GD221.4437.1]

MCQUEEN, JOHN, with his sister, from Portree, Skye, applied to emigrate to Australia in 1854. [NRS.GD221.4437.1]

MCQUEEN, Mrs MARGARET MARTIN, a widow in Skye, with her children Flora, Alexander, Donald, and Angus, emigrated to Wilmington, North Carolina, in 1802, settled in Moore County.

MCQUEEN, Mrs MARGARET, from Skye, died in North Carolina on 5 September 1837, buried in Stewartsville cemetery, Laurenburg, Scotland County, N.C. [Laurinburg gravestone]

MCQUEEN, PETER, born 1763 on Skye, son of Reverend William McQueen and his wife Nancy Isabella Campbell, emigrated to Wilmington, North Carolina, in 1802, settled in Moore County.

MCQUEEN, PETER, born 1812, Jane born 1816, John born 1839, Alexander born 1846, and Kenneth born 1849, from Glen Skeabost, Skye, emigrated via Glasgow on board the Georgiana bound for Port Philip, Australia, on 13 July 1852. [NRS.HD4/5]

MCQUIEN, NEIL, son of Janet McQuien in Bracadale, [Bracadal], Skye, was accused of theft in 1840. [NRS.AD14.40.16]

MACQUILKAN, SWENE, at Ardminish, [Aird Mheanais], Gigha, in 1849. [NRS.SC50.5.1849.3]

MCRAE, ANGUS, tenant in Durinish, [Diuranais], Skye, 1809. [NRS.GD23.6.456]

MCRAE, DUNCAN, born 16 November 1829 in North Uist, son of Reverend Finlay McRae and his wife Isabella McDonald, emigrated to Australia, died in 1866. [F.7.192]

MCRAE, JOHN, born 1826, with Ann born 1832, from Carbost, Skye, emigrated via Glasgow on board the Georgiana bound for Port Philip, Australia, on 13 July 1852. [NRS.HD4/5]

MCRAE, MALCOLM, born 1803, wife Helen born 1813, Christopher born 35, John born 37, Duncan born 1839, Janet born 1842, Donald born 1844, Farquhar born 1847, Malcolm born 1850, from Uig, emigrated to Port Philip, Australia, aboard the Ticonderoga in 1852. [NRS.HD4.5]

MCRITCHIE, KENNETH, born 1804 on Lewis, died 17 February 1885, husband of Catherine born 1807 on Lewis, died 14 September 1863. [Little Narrows Cemetery, Victoria County, Nova Scotia]

MCRITCHIE, MALCOLM, born 1795 on Lewis, died 13 August 1883. [Little Narrows Cemetery, Victoria County, Nova Scotia]

MCSUINE, DONALD, probably from Skye, died in Cumberland County, North Carolina, in 1809, probate December 1809, N.C. [NCSA.WBA.144]

PEOPLE OF THE HEBRIDES, 1800-1850

MCSWEEN, ALEXANDER, with his wife and four children, a cottar on the farm of Kingsburgh, [Cinnseborg], Skye, emigrated to Australia on the Arabian in 1854. [NRS.GD371.241.1]

MCSWEEN, ANGUS, born 1818, Isabella born 1820, Donald born 1846, John born 1849, and Neil born 1851, from Dunvegan, Skye, emigrated via Liverpool on board the Arabian bound for Victoria, Australia, on 27 October 1852. [NRS.HD.4/5]

MCSWEEN, ANGUS, with one son and two daughters, from Kingsburgh, Skye, applied to emigrate to Australia in 1854. [NRS.GD221.4437.1]

MCSWEEN, DONALD, a tenant of Lord MacDonald in Upper Oilach, Skye, bound for America around 1802. [NRS.GD221.4433.1]

MCSWEEN, DONALD, born 1812, Ann born 1808, Effy born 1837, John born 1839, Ann born 1841, Christy born 1845, Neil born 1847, and Mary born 1851, from Camuslenevaig, [Camas Dionabhavaig], Skye, emigrated via Liverpool on board the Priscilla bound for Victoria, Australia, on 15 October 1852. [NRS.HD4/5]

MCSWEEN, JOHN, born 1802 on Barra, died at Beaver Cove, Cape Breton, on 10 December 1894, Mary, his wife, born 1813 on Barra, died 1 February 1895. [St Andrew's RC Cemetery, Boisdale, Cape Breton.]

MCTAGGART, ARCHIBALD, born 1822, a tenant in Upper Killean, parish of Oa, Islay, with his wife born 1832, Catherine born 1853, Christina born 1855, and Duncan born 1859, emigrated via Glasgow on board the Damascus bound for Toronto, Canada, on 28 June 1862. [JRK]

MACTAGGART, MALCOLM, a labourer in Bunanuilt, Islay, was accused of murder in 1819. [NRS.AD14.19.310]

130

MCTAVISH, ARCHIBALD, minister of Jura and Colonsay, letters, 1811-1813. [NRS.GD64.180-181]

MCTAVISH, COLIN, a surgeon in Spring Bank, Killarow, [Cill A Rubha], Islay, 1837. [NRS.AD14.37.194]

MANSON, JOHN, a wool merchant at Kyleakin, [Caol Acain], Skye, in 1832. [NRS.CS96.172]

MARK, GEORGE, a merchant in Bowmore, Islay, an edict of executry, 13 October 1802. [NRS.CC12.3.7/5]

MARTIN, ALEXANDER, born 1813, Elizabeth born 1812, Samuel born 1839, and Ann born 1841, from Glasphern, [Glas Pheighinn], Skye, emigrated via Liverpool aboard the Allison bound for Melbourne, Australia, on 13 September 1852. [NRS.HD4/5]

MARTIN, CHARLES, tutor in law of John McDougall Martin, to sell land in Tobermory, Mull, 1830. [NRS.CS46.1830.143]

MARTIN, DONALD, born 1759 in Sizort, Skye, emigrated aboard the Polly in 1803, settled at Point Prim and on the Newtown River, Prince Edward Island, died 1848. [SP]

MARTIN, DONALD, from Skye, emigrated via Greenock aboard the Portaferry bound for Quebec in 1832. [Quebec Mercury, 13.6.1832]

MARTIN, DONALD ARCHIBALD, born on 3 August 1855 in Snizort and Uig, Skye, son of Reverend Angus Martin and his wife Margaret Nicolson, settled in British Columbia. [F.7.180]

MARTIN, JOHN, born 1805, Annabella born 1806, Mary born 1832, Marion born 1832, Jessie born 1834, Margaret born 1837, Abigail born 1839, Charles born 1842, John born 1844, and Allan born 1849, from Lonefearn, emigrated via Liverpool aboard the Araminta bound for Geelong, Australia, on 20 June 1852. [NRS.HD4/5]

MARTIN, JOHN LACHLAN, born 10 March 1847, in Snizort and Uig, Skye, son of Reverend Angus Martin and his wife Margaret Nicolson, died in India. [F.7.180]

MARTIN, MARTIN, a tenant of Lord MacDonald in Balmeanach, Skye, bound for America around 1802. [NRS.GD221.4433.1]

MARTIN, MARTIN, born 3 September 1853, in Snizort and Uig, Skye, son of Reverend Angus Martin and his wife Margaret Nicolson, died in India. [F.7.180]

MARTIN, MARTIN, and his sister, from Erlish, Skye, applied to emigrate to Australia in 1854. [NRS.GD221.4437.1]

MARTIN, SAMUEL MCDONALD, born 11 November 1850, in Snizort and Uig, Skye, son of Reverend Angus Martin and his wife Margaret Nicolson, emigrated to Australia. [F.7.180]

MARTIN, WILLIAM, in Oze, [Ose], Skye, a petition re Donald Nicolson in Clachgarach, Scorrybreck, Portree, Skye, dated 30 September 1822. [NRS.CC12.6.9.14]; he was granted a bond of caution in 1822 by William McLeod of Feorlig now in Stein and by Olaus McLeod of Fasach. [NRS.CC12.8.1.24]

MATHESON, ALEXANDER, born 1806, his wife born 1812, Isabella born 1836, Dugald born 1837, his wife born 1840, Margaret born 1842, Catherine born 1841, and Janet born 1835, from Islay, emigrated via Glasgow on board the Damascus bound for Toronto, Canada, on 28 June 1862. [JRK]

MATHESON, DONALD, born 1794 on Lewis, died 8 April 1869, husband of Ellen born 1803 on Lewis, died 16 April 1869. [Little Narrows Cemetery, Victoria County. Nova Scotia]

MATHESON, DONALD, in Gralin, Kilmuir, [Cill Mhoire], Skye, accused of sheep-stealing in 1838. [NRS.AD14.38.23]

MATHESON, DONALD, born 1805, Christy born 1812, Catherine born 1832, Ann born 1835, John born 1839, and Angus born 1842, from Glasphin, [Glas Pheighinn], Skye, emigrated via

Liverpool on board the Priscilla bound for Victoria, Australia, on 15 October 1852. [NRS.HD4/5]

MATHESON, JOHN, born 1800 on Lewis, died 20 December 1869. [Little Narrows Cemetery, Victoria County. Nova Scotia]

MATHESON, JOHN, born 1807, Rachel born 1808, Mary born 1832, Jane born 1834, Marion born 1837, Flora born 1840, Alexander born 1845, and Christy born 1848, from Sconser, [Sgonnsar], Skye, emigrated via Liverpool aboard the Araminta bound for Geelong, Australia, on 20 June 1852. [NRS.HD4/5]

MATHESON, JOHN, born 1812, his wife born 1814, Catherine born 1841, Alexander born 1843, Eliza born 1846, John born 1848, Dugald born 1850, Barbara born 1854, Duncan born 1855, Isabella born 1856, and Janet born 1858, from Islay, emigrated via Glasgow on board the Damascus bound for Toronto, Canada, on 28 June 1862. [JRK]

MATHESON, MARY, born 1828, from Glasphen, [Glas Pheiginn], emigrated via Liverpool on board the Allison bound for Melbourne, Australia, on 13 September 1852. [NRS.HD4/5]

MATHESON, NEIL, on Prince Edward Island, versus Archibald McNiven, emigration agent in Tobermory, Mull, for injury and damages in 1830. [NRS.CS228.M13.13]

MATHESON, NEIL, born 1808, his wife born 1814, Isabella born 1840, Catherine born 1840, Donald born 1842, Duncan born 1846, Martha 1850, James born 1854, and Mary born 1856, from Islay, emigrated via Glasgow on board the Damascus bound for Toronto, Canada, on 28 June 1862. [JRK]

MAXWELL, JAMES, agent for the British Fishery Society in Tobermory, Mull, a letter, 1806. [NRS.GD9.60]; in Aros, Mull, factor for the Duke of Argyll, letters, 1801-1825. [NRS.HD174.1478/1647/1671]

MAXWELL, JOHN ARGYLE, in Portree, Skye, 1836.
[NRS.JC26.1836.103]

MENZIES, DUNCAN, born 1809, Margaret born 1811, Mary Ann born 1830, Jean born 1832, Margaret born 1834, Archibald born 1836, Scotia born 1838, Duncan born 1840, Catherine born 1842, Alexander born 1848, and Ann born 1851, from Ballygowan, [Baile a' Ghobhainn], Mull, emigrated via Liverpool on board the Marmion bound for Moreton Bay, Australia, on 28 August 1852. [NRS.HD4/5]

MILLOY, MARION, daughter of Archibald Milloy a farmer on Gigha in 1841. [NRS.SC50.5.1841.32]

MONRO, ALEXANDER, born 1834, from Uig, emigrated via Liverpool on board the Allison bound for Melbourne, Australia, on 13 September 1852. [NRS.HD4/5]

MONTGOMERY, GEORGE, a whisky distiller in Octomore, Islay, in 1818.

MORRISON, ALEXANDER, born 1767 on Lewis died 2 December 1843, husband of Christina, born 1792 on Lewis, died 7 October 1856. [MacLeod Pioneer Cemetery, Richmond County, Nova Scotia]

MORRISON, ALEXANDER, postmaster at Dunvegan, Skye, 1802. [NRS.NRAS.2177.1512]

MORRISON, ALEXANDER, born 1803, Flora born 1811, Mary born 1834, Peggy born 1835, Donald born 1838, Effy born 1841, and John born 1842, emigrated via Tobermory, Mull, on board the Catherine of Belfast on 13 July 1843, transferred to the John and Robert bound from Belfast, Ireland, in September 1843, and landed at the Gut of Canso, Cape Breton. [PANS.CS88.M112]

MORRISON, ALEXANDER, in Eyre, [Eighre], Raasay, applied to emigrate to Australia in 1854. [NRS.GD221.4437.1]

MORRISON, ANGUS, born 1797, of Uig, Lewis, was accused of housebreaking and theft at Stein, Durinish, [Diuranais], Skye, in 1823. [NRS.AD14.23.231]

MORRISON, CHARLES, born 1843, emigrated from Harris aboard the Clansman bound for Australia in 1857. [NRS.GD371.241.1]

MORRISON, DONALD, born 1786 on Skye, died near Galatia Church, North Carolina, on 28 May 1862. [NCPresbyterian]

MORISON, DONALD, tenant of Ferinardry, Ulva, in 1824. [NRS.GD174.1140.9]

MORRISON, DONALD, born 1789, Flora born 1804, Mary born 1828, Donald born 1832, Jane born 1836, Kenneth born 1839, Catherine born 1841, and Christy born 1844, from North Uist, emigrated via Greenock aboard the Cashmere of Glasgow bound for Quebec in 1849. [NRS.GD221.4011.53]

MORRISON, DONALD, born 1807, wife Effy born 1811, children Marion born 1834, Christina born 1837, Angus born 1839, Catherine born 1841, Charles born 1843,Margaret born 1843, John born 1845, Ann born 1849, Christina born 1853, emigrated from Harris aboard the Clansman bound for Australia on 13 July 1857. [NRS.GD371.241.1][NRS.HD4/5]

MORRISON, DONALD, and his wife Barbara White, were parents of Diana baptised on Handa, [Eilean Shannda], in 1823, and of Christian baptised on Handa in 1825. [HS.20.5]

MORRISON, DONALD, born 1817, Ann born 1827, Ann born 1847, Marion born 1849, and Allan born 1856, emigrated from Harris on board the Clansman bound for Australia on 13 July 1857. [NRS.GD371.241.1]

MORRISON, FINLAY, born 1802, Christina born 1831, John born 1832, Kenneth born 1847, and Angus born 1852, emigrated from Harris on board the Clansman bound for Australia on 13 July 1857. [NRS.GD371.241.1]

MORISON, HUGH, a tenant in Kilbeg, Mull, a letter, 1798. [NRS.GD174.1389.35]

MORRISON, HUGH, born 1827, wife Mary born 1831, Catherine born 1854, and Murdoch born 1856, emigrated from Harris [Na Hearadh], aboard the Clansman on 13 July 1857 bound for Australia. [NRS.GD371.241.1]

MORRISON, HUGH, born 1815, Catherine born 1815, John born 1840, Duncan born 1842, Angus born 1845, Salvia born 1849, and Malcolm born 1853, emigrated from Harris on board the Clansman bound for Australia on 13 July 1857. [NRS.GD371.241.1]

MORRISON, JAMES, born 1781 on Mull, died in South Carolina on 14 October 1819. [Old Scots gravestone, Charleston, S.C.]

MORRISON, JANET, a young girl from Lyndale, Skye, applied to emigrate to Australia in 1854. [NRS.GD221.4437.1]

MORRISON, JOHN, born 1799 on Lewis, [Leodhas], died 17 September 1868, husband of Sarah, born 1807 on Lewis, died 14 March 1889. [Morrison Cemetery, Cape Breton]

MORRISON, JOHN, born 24 December 1804 on Lewis, died 22 November 1900, husband of Catherine, born 1815 on Lewis, died 23 October 1877. [Little Narrows Cemetery, Victoria County, Nova Scotia]

MORISON, JOHN, tenant of Cragaig, Crachdaig], Ulva, in 1824. [NRS.GD174.1140.9]

MORRISON, JOHN, born 1766, was drowned in the Sound of Iona on 2 May 1828, husband of Jessie Maclean, born 1787, died 16 May 1869. [Kilvickeon gravestone, Mull]

MORRISON, JOHN, a blacksmith in Bowmore, Islay, in 1845. [NRS.SC50.5.1845.3]

MORRISON, JOHN, born 1812, Salvia born 1815, John born 1833, Ann born 1839, Rachel born 1841, Ewen born 1843, Christina born 1847, John born 1852, and Marjory born 1854, emigrated from Harris on board the Clansman bound for Australia on 13 July 1857. [NRS.GD371.241.1]

MORRISON, KENNETH, probably from Lewis, settled in British Columbia by 1859. [NLS.Acc.6879]

MORISON, MAGNUS, born 1793, son of Charles Morison the tacksman of Ballachry, died 23 June 1811. [Kilmore Dervaig gravestone, Mull]

MORRISON, MARGARET, born 1834, emigrated from Harris on board the Clansman bound for Australia on 13 July 1857. [NRS.GD371.241.1]

MORRISON, MARION, from South Uist, emigrated aboard the Emperor Alexander of Aberdeen, master Alexander Watt, from Tobermory, Mull, to Sydney, Cape Breton, in July 1823, landed on 16 September 1823. [Inverness Journal, 30 January 1824]

MORRISON, MARY, born 1795, from St Kilda, emigrated via Liverpool on board the Priscilla bound for Victoria, Australia, on 15 October 1852. [NRS.HD4/5]

MORRISON, MURDOCH, born 1830, with Christina born 1831, and Effie born 1856, emigrated from Harris aboard the Clansman bound for Australia in 1857. [NRS.GD371.241.1]

MORRISON, ROBERT, in Stornaway, Lewis, [Steornabhagh, Leodhas], later in Mississippi, letters, 1826-1855, [NRS.GD403.68]

MORISON, RODERICK, tenant of Upper Kilvickewan, [Cill Mhic Eoghann], Ulva, in 1824. [NRS.GD174.1140.9]

MORISON, Dr RODERICK, in Bridgeport, Mississippi, a letter to his cousin Mrs Annabella McKenzie in Dunvegan, Skye, dated 20 March 1840. [NRS.GD403.68.7]

MUNDEL, JOHN, born 1797, Kate born 1809, Hector born 1829, Mary born 1831, and John born 1837, from North Uist, emigrated via Greenock aboard the Waterhen of London bound for Quebec in 1849. [NRS.GD221.4435]

MUNN, ANGUS, born 1774 on Colonsay, died on Prince Edward Island on 27 July 1837. [Woods Islands Pioneer Cemetery, P.E.I.]

MUNN, JAMES, born 1781 on Colonsay, emigrated to Prince Edward Island in 1812, died in Pictou, Nova Scotia, in 1833. [Woods Island Pioneer Cemetery, P.E.I.]

MUNN, JOHN, born 1760, a labourer from Colonsay, [Colbhasa], with his wife Catherine born 1766, and children Donald born 1792, Duncan born 1794, Sarah born 1796, Catherine born 1801, Barbara born 1803, and John born 1804, emigrated from Oban aboard the Clarendon of Hull, bound for Charlottetown, Prince Edward Island, in August 1808. [TNA.CO226.23]

MUNN, JOHN, born on Colonsay in 1802, emigrated to Prince Edward Island in 1812, died in Pictou, Nova Scotia, in 1833. [Woods Island Pioneer Cemetery]

MUNRO, JOHN, a merchant in Bowmore, Islay, [Bogha Mor, Ile], 1836. [NRS.CS228.R11.32/2]

MUNRO, WILLIAM, a writer in Portree, Skye, a bond of caution to Catherine Shaw in Uig, Isle of Lewis, [Leodhas], executor to Angus Shaw of Ballimore in Durinish, [Diuranais], 9 January 1821. [NRS.CC12.8.1.21]

MURCHISON, ALEXANDER, born 1810, Catherine born 1817, Hugh born 1848, and Flora born 1851, from Bernisdale,

[Bearnasdal], Skye, emigrated via Liverpool aboard the Priscilla bound for Victoria, Australia, on 15 October 1852. [NRS.HD4/5]

MURRAY, JOHN, on Eigg, letters, 1823. [NRS.GD47.713]

NAPIER, JOHN, in Ardelamy, Gigha, 1841. [NRS.SC50.841.59]

NEILSON, CATHERINE, born 1799, from North Uist, emigrated via Greenock aboard the Waterhen of London bound for Quebec in 1849. [NRS.GD221.4435]

NICHOLSON, ALEXANDER, born 1780 on Skye, died on Prince Edward Island on 26 September 1820. [Polly cemetery, Belfast, P.E.I.]

NICHOLSON, ALEXANDER, with Margaret, and sons John and Donald, from Skye aboard the Malay bound for Sydney, Nova Scotia, in 1830. [NSARM.RG1.67/19]

NICHOLSON, ALEXANDER, born 1816, Mary born 1823, Alexander born 1844, John born 1846, Donald born 1849, and an infant, from Glen Skeabost, emigrated via Glasgow on board the Georgiana bound for Port Philip, Australia, on 13 July 1852. [NRS.HD4/5]

NICHOLSON, ANGUS in Portree, Skye, 1818. [NRS.AD14.18.89]

NICHOLSON, ANGUS, born 1809, wife Susan born 1818, children Alexander born 1841, John born 1846, and Catherine born 1844, from Uig, Skye, emigrated on the Ticonderoga bound for Port Philip, Australia, in 1852. [NRS.HD4/5]

NICHOLSON, CATHERINE, born 1802, Mary born 1833, and Donald born 1837, from Auchnahanait, emigrated via Liverpool on board the Priscilla bound for Victoria, Australia, on 15 October 1852. [NRS.HD4/5]

NICHOLSON, CHARLES, born 1796 on Skye, died on Prince Edward Island on 20 May 1864, husband of Mary, born 1800, died 23 May 1880. [Polly cemetery, Belfast, PEI.]

NICHOLSON, DONALD, born 1787 on Skye, died on Prince Edward Island in April 1883. [Polly cemetery, Belfast, PEI.]

NICHOLSON, DUNCAN, with Anne, from Skye aboard the Malay bound for Sydney, Nova Scotia, in 1830. [NSARM.RG1.67/19]

NICHOLSON, IAIN, with Anna MacNeil his wife, and children Iain born 1802, Flora, Uilleam, Mairi, Pol, and Ciorsdan, from Cliad, Barra, possibly emigrated on board the Harmony to Cape Breton in 1821.

NICHOLSON, JAMES, with Margaret and children Anne and John, from Skye aboard the Malay bound for Sydney, Nova Scotia, in 1830. [NSARM.RG1.67/19]

NICHOLSON, NIALL, with Mairi his wife, and children Mairi, Caitriona, Ciordan, Iain, and Mor, from Cleat, Barra, possibly emigrated on board the Harmony to Cape Breton in 1821.

NICHOLSON, SAMUEL, with Kate, and children John, Norman, Alexander, Mary, and Norman, from Skye aboard the Malay bound for Sydney, Nova Scotia, in 1830. [NSARM.RG1.67/19]

NICOL, JOHN, born 1802, from Banff, an Excise officer, died in Bowmore, Islay, in 1833. [Kilnaughton gravestone, Islay]

NICOLSON, ALEXANDER, in Benbecula, [Beinn nam Fadhla], a letter dated 19 March 1804. [NRS.NRAS.2177.1522]

NICOLSON, ALEXANDER, born 1827, son of Malcolm Nicolson of Husabost in the parish of Duirinish, Skye, a graduate of Edinburgh University, a lawyer and later Sheriff of Kirkcudbright, a Gaelic scholar, died 20 January 1893.

NICOLSON, ANGUS, a merchant in Portree, Skye, in 1828. [NRS.CS271.78]

NICOLSON, ANGUS, with his wife, one daughter, his sister, and an infant, from Balmeanach, Skye, emigrated on board the

Edward Johnstone bound for Australia in 1854. [NRS.GD371.241.1]

NICOLSON, ANN, a widow, with two sons and one daughter, from Coilliemore, Skye, applied to emigrate to Australia in 1854. [NRS.GD371.241.1]

NICOLSON, ARCHIE, and his sister, from Balgown, Skye, applied to emigrate to Australia in 1854. [NRS.GD371.241.1]

NICOLSON, MALCOLM, in Scorrebreck, Portree, Skye, a commission dated 18 August 1813. [NRS.CC12.3.7.253]

NICOLSON, MARION, from Tormichaig, Skye, applied to emigrate to Australia in 1854. [NRS.GD371.241.1]

NICOLSON, MARY, with two sons and two daughters, in Coilliemore, [Coille Mor], Skye, applied to emigrate to Australia in 1854. [NRS.GD221.4437.1]

NICOLSON, JOHN, in Stein, Durinish, [Diuranais], Skye, a victim of theft in 1823. [NRS.A14.23.231]

NICOLSON, JOHN, with his wife, two sons, and two daughters, from Camustianavaig, Skye, emigrated to Australia on board the Arabian in 1854. [NRS.GD371.241.1]

NICOLSON, PATRICK, in Tirluin, a letter concerning an emigrant ship at Barra dated 28 June 1802. [NRS.NRAS.2177.1512]

NICOLSON, SAMUEL, born 1815, Isabella born 1812, Donald born 1836, Alexander born 1838, Flora born 1840, Patrick born 1843, and Christian born 1846, from Garremore, [An Garradh Mor], emigrated via Liverpool aboard the Araminta bound for Geelong, Australia, on 20 June 1852. [NRS.HD4/5]

NICOLSON, WILLIAM, with his wife, two sons, three daughters, and his sister in law, from Balmeanach, Skye, applied to emigrate to Australia in 1854. [NRS.GD221.4437.1]

NICOLSON, Mrs, a widow, with one son, and a daughter, from Peinchorran, Skye, applied to emigrate to Australia in 1854. [NRS.GD371.241.1]

NICOLSON, WILLIAM, born on Lewis, [Leodhas], died 1862. [United Church Cemetery, Fox Harbour, Cumberland County, Nova Scotia]

NISBET, HENRY, born 1810, a banker and procurator fiscal in Tobermory, Mull, in 1843, died in 1867. [M.272/460]

NISBET, JAMES, agent for the British Fishery Society in Tobermory, Mull, a letter, 1827. [NRS.GD9.64]; victim of letter theft in 1828. [NRS.JC26.1828.397]

NIVEN, DONALD, in Conispy, Bridgend, Kilchoman, [Cill Chomain], Islay, was accused of murder in 1823. [NRS.AD14.23.42]

NOBLE, ANN, on Lismore, [Liosmor], a letter dated 14 June 1802. [NRS.NRAS.2177.1512]

O'HENLY, DUGALD, tenant of Lower Kilvickewan, Ulva, in 1824. [NRS.GD174.1140.9]

O'HENLY, JOHN, tenant of Lower Kilvickewan, [Cill Mhic Eoghainn], Ulva, in 1824. [NRS.GD174.1140.9]

O'HEULY, ANGUS, emigrated aboard the Emperor Alexander of Aberdeen, master Alexander Watt, from Tobermory, Mull, to Sydney, Cape Breton, in July 1823., landed on 16 September 1823. [Inverness Journal, 30 January 1824]

O'HEULY, JOHN, from South Uist, emigrated aboard the Emperor Alexander of Aberdeen, master Alexander Watt, from Tobermory, Mull, to Sydney, Cape Breton, in July 1823, landed on 16 September 1823. [Inverness Journal, 30 January 1824]

O'HEULY, RANALD, emigrated aboard the Emperor Alexander of Aberdeen, master Alexander Watt, from Tobermory, Mull, to Sydney, Cape Breton, in July 1823, landed on 16 September 1823. [Inverness Journal, 30 January 1824]

PATERSON, JAMES, a mason on Harris, a decreet, 1819. [NRS.CS40.31.58]

PORTER, Dr WILLIAM, agent of the British Fisheries Society at Lochbay, [Loch a Bhaigh], Skye, in a letter dated 27 December 1802, claimed that *9,700 have migrated to Carolina, Canada, and Nova Scotia since the Peace'*. [NRS.GD9.166.23/3]; letters from 1801 to 1804. [NRS.GD9.159]

RAMSAY, JAMES, of the Port Ellen Distillery, Islay, 1836.

RANKIN, C. D., born 1777, Flora born 1782, George born 1806, from Tobermory, Mull, aboard the brig Humphreys bound for Prince Edward Island in 1806. [PAPEI.2702]

RITCHIE, ALEXANDER, mate of the Revenue cutter Royal George testament confirmed in 1804, Commissariat of the Isles. [NRS.CC12.7.23]

ROBERTSON, ALEXANDER, born 1810, Marion born 1810, Betsy born 1832, Charles born 1834, Christian born 1839, Lachlan born 1841, and William born 1844, from Elgol, [Ealaghol], Skye, emigrated via Liverpool aboard the Araminta bound for Geelong, Australia, on 20 June 1852. [NRS.HD4/5]

ROBERTSON, ANGUS, born 1799, Helen born 1799, Alexander born 1825, Angus born 1834, and Charles born 1838, emigrated via Liverpool aboard the Araminta bound for Geelong, Australia, on 20 June 1852. [NRS.HD4/5]

ROBERTSON, CHARLES, at Dunvegan, Skye, agent for the British Fishery Society, letters, 1808-1809. [NRS.GD9.194]

ROBERTSON, JOHN, born 1814, Ann born 1813, with John born 1836, from Uig, emigrated via Liverpool on board the Allison bound for Melbourne, Australia, on 1 September 1852. [NRS.HD4/5]

ROBERTSON, NEIL, born 1807, Isabella born 1809, John born 1827, Margaret born 1833, Christy born 1837, Jane born 1840, Kate born 1841, Archibald born 1843, Donald born 1846, and Kate born 1817, from Camuscross, [Camas Cros], Skye, emigrated via Liverpool aboard the Arabian bound for Victoria, Australia, on 27 October 1852. [NRS.HD4/5]

ROSE, JOHN, miller in Kilmaluaig, 1812. [NRS.AD14.12.36]

ROSS, ALEXANDER, son of Lauchlin Ross and his wife Catherine Martin in Strath, Skye, emigrated to Prince Edward Island in 1821. [SP]

ROSS, ALEXANDER, with Anne and children Mary, John, Donald, Bain, and Flora, from Skye aboard the Malay bound for Sydney, Nova Scotia, in 1830. [NSARM.RG1.67/19]

ROSS, DAVID, born 1805, minister of Tobermory from 1844 until 1855, died 1891. [M.460]

ROSS, DAVID, born 1810, son of Lauchlan Ross and his wife Catherine Martin in Strath, Skye, emigrated to Prince Edward Island in 1821, married Anne Martin, died 10 December 1890. [SP]

ROSS, DONALD, born 27 July 1804, son of Lauchlan Ross and his wife Catherine Martin in Strath, Skye, emigrated to Prince Edward Island in 1821, married Flora Nicolson, died 9 December 1856. [SP]

ROSS, DONALD, with Kate and children Kate, Margaret, and Mary, from Skye aboard the Malay bound for Sydney, Nova Scotia, in 1830. [NSARM.RG1.67/19]

ROSS, DONALD, and his wife, from Conordan, Skye, emigrated to Australia aboard the Arabian in 1854. [NRS.GD221.4437.1]

ROSS, EWEN, born 1812, Mary born 1822, Niel born 1846, Mary born 1848, and Alexander born 1850, from Duntolin, [Dun Thuilm], Skye, emigrated via Liverpool on board the Allison bound for Melbourne, Australia, on 13 September 1852. [NRS.HD4/5]

ROSS, EWEN, and his wife, from Conordan, [An Comhnardan], Skye, emigrated to Australia aboard the Arabian in 1854. [NRS.GD221.4437.1]

ROSS, HUGH, born 1812, Ann born 1810, Ann born 1833, Catherine born 1837, Isabella born 1839, Alexander born 1841, and Duncan born 1845, from Uig, emigrated via Liverpool on board the Priscilla bound for Victoria, Australia, on 15 October 1852. [NRS.HD4/5]

ROSS, ISABEL, daughter of Lauchlan Ross and his wife Catherine Martin, in Strath, [Srath MhicFhionghain], Skye, emigrated to Prince Edward Island in 1821. [SP]

ROSS, JOHN, a tenant of Lord MacDonald in Kendram, Skye, bound for America around 1802. [NRS.GD221.4433.1]

ROSS, JOHN, with Mary, from Skye aboard the Malay bound for Sydney, Nova Scotia, in 1830. [NSARM.RG1.67/19]

ROSS, JOHN, with Mary and children Mary, Angus, Christy, Bell, and Murdo, from Skye aboard the Malay bound for Sydney, Nova Scotia, in 1830. [NSARM.RG1.67/19]

ROSS, JOHN, his wife, and six sons, from Portree, Skye, applied to emigrate to Australia in 1854. [NRS.GD221.4437.1]

ROSS LAUCHLAN, born 1770 in Strath, Skye, with his wife Catherine Martin, and children, emigrated to Prince Edward Island in 1821, died on 15 July 1848. [SP]

ROSS, LACHLAN, born 1824, his wife born 1817, Lachlan born 1835, William born 1837, Helen born 1840, Anne born 1843, Flora born 1847, and Norman born 1851, from Swordale, Skye, emigrated via Liverpool aboard the Araminta bound for Geelong, Australia, on 20 June 1852. [NRS.HD4/5]

ROSS, LACHLAN, born 1828, his wife Isabella Buchanan, and William born 1850, from Broadford, [An t-Ath Leathann], Skye, emigrated via Glasgow, to Port Phillip, Australia, aboard the Georgiana on 13 July 1852. [NRS.4/5]

ROSS, WALTER, born 1820, son of Lauchlan Ross and his wife Catherine Martin in Strath, [An Srath], Skye, emigrated to Prince Edward Island in 1821, married Catherine Murchison, settled in Eldon, died 29 March 1875. [SP]

SCOTT, EDWARD H., in North Harris, an inventory, 18... [NRS.GD1.1159]

SHAW, ALEXANDER, born 1809, Marian born 1814, Alexander born 1846, and John born 1850, from Portree, Mull, emigrated via Liverpool on board the Thames bound for Melbourne, Australia, on 3 November 1852. [NRS.HD4/5]

SHAW, ANGUS, innkeeper in Dunvegan, Skye, letters, 1791-1802. [NRS.GD9.110]

SHAW, DUNCAN, in Dunvegan, Skye, a letter, 1811. [NRS.GD23.6.492]

SHAW, DUNCAN, in Benbecula, [Beinn nam Fadhla], factor of the Harris estate, a letter, 1830, [NRS.GD29.5.1232]; a letter 1836. [NRS.GD46.13.45]

SHAW, EDWARD, a tailor employed by Dugald McLachlan a merchant tailor in Tobermory, Mull, was tried for housebreaking in 1827. [NRS.JC26.1827.164]

SHAW, JOHN, born 1809, Margaret born 1819, Ann born 1835, Alexander born 1837, John born 1839, Christina born 1841, Angus born 1845, Catherine born 1843, Mary born 1849, Hanna born 1852, and John born 1854, emigrated from Harris on board the Clansman bound for Australia on 13 July 1857. [NRS.GD371.241.1]

SHIELLS, ALEXANDER, from Earlston, Berwickshire, factor and overseer at Torluisk, Mull, from 1822 to 1830s. [M.460]

SIMSON, HECTOR, in Bowmore, [Bogha Mor], Islay, a deed, 1821. [NRS.GD64.1.258]

SIMSON, WILLIAM, acting Customs collector at in Bowmore, Islay, a deed, 1821. [NRS.GD64.1.258]

SINCLAIR, ALEXANDER, a farmer in Erray, [Earraid], Mull, in 1843. [M.274]

SINCLAIR, DONALD, on Islay, versus John Sinclair on Islay, in June 1829. [NRS.CS44.175.52]

SINCLAIR, JOHN, born 1770, a merchant and distiller in Tobermory, Mull, was granted a charter of land in Morvern in 1822. [NRS.GD218.180-182][M.460]

SINCLAIR, JOHN, shepherd at Beneila, husband of Catherine, born 1762, died 1 July 1831. [Killean, Loch Spelve, gravestone, Mull]

SKINNER, MARY, born 1761, from Tobermory, Mull, aboard the brig Isle of Skye bound for Prince Edward Island in 1806. [PAPEI.2702]

SMITH, DAVID, tenant of Kinerach, Gigha, 1838. [NRS.SC50.5.1838.12]

SMITH, DONALD, born 1742 on Colonsay, [Colbhasa], emigrated to Prince Edward Island in 1820, died there on 19 March 1875. [Woods Island Pioneer Cemetery, P.E.I.]

SMITH, DONALD, a cottar at Braehead of Ardminish, [Aird Mheanais], Gigha, 1849. [NRS.SC50.5.1849.5]

SMITH, JAMES, son of Archibald Smith a farmer on Gigha in 1841. [NRS.SC50.5.1841.32]

SMITH, JOHN, with wife Mary, and children Neil, John, Jean, and Mary, from Kildonan, [Cill Donnain], Islay, emigrated aboard the Prince of Wales bound for the Red River Settlement, Canada, in 1813. [PAC.M155,165-168]

SMITH, JOHN, emigrated aboard the Emperor Alexander of Aberdeen, master Alexander Watt, from Tobermory, Mull, to Sydney, Cape Breton, in July 1823., landed on 16 September 1823. [Inverness Journal, 30 January 1824]

SMITH, JOHN, junior, a crofter in Doune Carloway, [Dun Charlabhaigh], Uig, Lewis, accused of fraud in 1848. [NRS.AD14.48.186]

SMITH, MALCOLM, in Uigin, Uig, Lewis, accused of stealing sheep in 1847. [NRS.AD14.47.530]

SMITH, MERRAN, widow of Donald Smith a crofter at Ardminish, [Aird Mheanais], Gigha, 1839. [NRS.SC50.1839.18]

SMITH, NEIL, tenant of part of Aros, Mull, in 1838. [NRS.C50.5.1838.38]

SMITH, WILLIAM, a carpenter in Dunvegan, Skye, accounts, 1824. [NRS.GD46.1.456]

STEELE, ALASDAIR, from South Uist, possibly emigrated on board the Harmony to Cape Breton in 1821.

STEEL, ALEXANDER, emigrated aboard the Emperor Alexander of Aberdeen, master Alexander Watt, from Tobermory, Mull, to Sydney, Cape Breton, in July 1823, landed on 16 September 1823. [Inverness Journal, 30 January 1824]

STEEL, JOHN, emigrated aboard the Emperor Alexander of Aberdeen, master Alexander Watt, from Tobermory, Mull, to Sydney, Cape Breton, in July 1823., landed on 16 September 1823. [Inverness Journal, 30 January 1824]

STEELE, JOHN, born 1802 on South Uist, died 5 October 1865. [St Andrew's RC Cemetery, Boisdale, Cape Breton]

STEEL, RORY, a former servant, emigrated from Uist to Prince Edward Island in 1791, a letter to Colin MacDonald of Boisdale. [NLS.Adv.ms.73.2.13f]

STEWART, ALEXANDER, born 1798 on Skye, died on Prince Edward Island on 27 February 1890, his wife Catherine born 1813 on Skye, died 6 February 1883. [Little Sands cemetery, PEI]

STEWART, ALEXANDER, born 1819, Rachel born 1824, and Elspet born 1848, from North Uist, emigrated via Greenock aboard the Waterhen of London bound for Quebec in 1849. [NRS.GD221.4435]

STEWART, ALLAN, tacksman of Shuna, an edict of executry in 1800. [NRS.CC2.8.104.6]

STEWART, ARCHIBALD, in Scudaburgh [Sgudabrog] by Portree, letters 1833-1835. [NRS.GD46.1.316]

STEWART, DONALD, factor of Harris, 1830. [NRS.CS46.1830.8.12]

STEWART, DONALD, with his wife, three sons and two daughters, from Peinmore, [Am Peighinn Mor], Skye, applied to emigrate to Australia in 1854. [NRS.GD221.4437.1]

STEWART, DUNCAN, in Bein Luskintyre, Harris, was accused of sheep stealing in 1836. [NRS.AD14.36.38]

STEWART, DUNCAN, born 1809, with wife Janet born 1815, Catherine born 1841, and John born 1843, from North Uist, emigrated via Greenock aboard the <u>Cashmere of Glasgow</u> bound for Quebec in 1849. [NRS.GD221.4011.53]

STEWART, ISABELLA, born 1795, daughter of Robert Stewart of Achadashenaig, wife of Dugald McLachlan, died 1869. [M.233/461]

STEWART, JOHN, minister of Lismore, [Liosmor], a letter, 1804. [NRS.GD13.420]; born 1757, minister of Lismore for 35 years, died 13 July 1837. [Lismore gravestone]

STEWART, JOHN, a linen weaver in Keills, Islay, in 1828. [I.247]

STEWART, JOHN, with Christy and children Kate and Janet, from Skye aboard the <u>Malay</u> bound for Sydney, Nova Scotia, in 1830. [NSARM.RG1.67/19]

STEWART, JOHN, born 1790, of Achadashenaig, Mull, in 1843, died 1843. [M.274/461]

STEWART, JOHN, with his family, from Portree, Skye, applied to emigrate to Australia in 1854. [NRS.GD221.4437.1]

STEWART, JOHN, with his wife, two sons, and three daughters, from Camustinaveg, Skye, applied to emigrate to Australia in 1854. [NRS.GD221.4437.1]

STEWART, LACHLAN, born 1752, tenant of Lettermore, died in November 1834, husband of Ann McPhail, born 1767, died June 1852. [Glen Aros gravestone, Mull]

STEWART, NORMAN, with his wife and an infant, from Camustinaveg, [Camas Dionabhaig], Skye, applied to emigrate to Australia in 1854. [NRS.GD221.4437.1]

STEWART, PETER, with Margaret and son Allan, from Skye aboard the <u>Malay</u> bound for Sydney, Nova Scotia, in 1830. [NSARM.RG1.67/19]

STEWART, ROBERT, of the Marines, eldest son of the late Allan Stewart, tacksman of Shuna, Lismore, and his wife Mary McDonald, petitioned to open and inventory the repositories of his father on 1 April 1800, which was granted. [NRS.CC2.7.47.4]

STEWART, Lieutenant ROBERT, tenant in Achamore, [an t-Achad Mor], Gigha, 1839. [NRS.SC50.1839.18]

STEWART, ROBERT, of Achadashenaig, Mull, died in 1813. [M.195]

STEWART, RONALD D., born 1827 on Skye, died on Prince Edward Island on 15 October 1896. [Little Sands gravestone, PEI]

STUART, ALEXANDER, and Mary with children Donald, Agnes, Anne, Janet, and John, from Skye aboard the Malay bound for Sydney, Nova Scotia, in 1830. [NSARM.RG1.67/19]

TELFER, HUGH, in Skerrols near Bowmore, [Bogha Mor],Islay, a prisoner in Paisley Jail, suspension and liberation in 1844. [NRS.CS234.T24.5]

TELFER, JAMES, a tenant farmer in Skerrols, Islay, 1838.

THOMSON, DONALD, miller at Banegrunel, Lismore, [Liosmor], a petition, 1803. [NRS.GD170.564]

TOLMIE, ALLAN, born in April 1842, son of John Tolmie, tacksman of Uiginish in Skye, and his wife Margaret Hope MacAskill, died in October 1917 in New Zealand. [Dunvegan gravestone]

TOLMIE, BARBARA, daughter of John Tolmie of Uiginish, Skye, and his wife Jean McKenzie, wife of John McDonald tacksman of Scalpaig, [Sgalpaigh], Uist, letters 1808-1856. [NRS.GD403.65]

TOLMIE, DONALD, in Carbost, Skye, letters, 1848. [NRS.HD0.36]

TOLMIE, DONALD ALLAN, born in May 1828, son of John Tolmie, tacksman of Uiginish in Skye, and his wife Margaret Hope MacAskill, died in February 1900 in New Zealand. [Dunvegan gravestone]

TOLMIE, JOHN, postmaster at Dunvegan, [Dun Mheagain], Skye, 1793-1810. [NRS.GD403.41]

TOLMIE, JOHN, in Uigmisk, Skye, victim of a crime in 1837. [NRS.AD14.37.35]

TOLMIE, JOHN, in Uiginish, Skye, a letter to Hugh McAskill in Tallisker, [Talaisgeir], Skye, dated 1844. [NRS.GD403.78]

TOLMIE, MALCOLM, born in September 1836, son of John Tolmie, tacksman of Uiginish, [Uiginis], in Skye, and his wife Margaret Hope MacAskill, died 1904 in Australia. [Dunvegan gravestone]

TOLMIE, WILLIAM, Ensign of the Skye Battalion of Volunteer Infantry, 16 November 1804. [NRS.GD403.61.8]

TOLMIE, WILLIAM ALEXANDER, born in March 1833, son of John Tolmie, tacksman of Uiginish in Skye, and his wife Margaret Hope MacAskill, died in August 1875 in New Zealand. [Dunvegan gravestone]

TORRIE, ALEXANDER, tenant at Nisibost, Harris, a decreet, 1819. [NRS.CS40.31.58]

WALKER, WILLIAM, a linen weaver in Keills, Islay, in 1828. [I.247]

WATT, JAMES, a fisherman in Port Askaig, [Port Ascaig], Islay, master of the Rena of Islay in 1848. [NRS.SC50.5.1848.5]

WEBSTER, WILLIAM, overseer for Islay and factor of the Campbells' Woodhill Estate in Daill in 1838; in Daill, Islay, in 1848. [NRS.SC50.5.1848.5]; a sheep farmer in 1840s-1850s, having cleared the land of small farmers. [I.219]

WHITE, CHRISTY, born 1816, estranged wife of John White a porter, a servant to John Kennedy, tenant of Glenstockadale, Lismore, was accused of infanticide in 1843. [NRS.AD14.366]

WHYTE, GEORGE, from Fife, a farmer at Kilchiaran in the Rhinns, Islay, 1826.

WHYTE, ROBERT, a linen weaver in Keills, Islay, in 1828. [I.247]

WILLIAMS, SAMUEL MAY, born 1774, with Maria Williams born 1777, from Tobermory, Mull, [Tobar Mhoire], aboard the brig Humphreys bound for Prince Edward Island in 1806. [PAPEI.2702]

WILSON, GEORGE, in Callumkill, Islay, a sequestration petition, 1849. [NRS.CS279.2854]

YOUNG, ANDREW, a linen weaver in Keills, Islay, in 1828. [I.247]

YOUNG, WILLIAM, formerly an earthenware manufacturer in Glasgow and Jamaica, residing in Balygrant, Islay, was accused of homicide in 1815. [NRS.AD14.15.21]

REFERENCES

AJ   Aberdeen Journal, series

CMN   The Clan McNeill, [New York, 1923]

CS   Carolina Scots, [Dillon, S.C., 1998]

EEC   Edinburgh Evening Courant, series

F   Fasti Ecclesiae Scoticinae, [Edinburgh]

GM   Gentleman's Magazine, series

HS   History Scotland, series

I   Islay, the land of the Lordship, [Edinburgh, 2017]

IR   Innes Review, [series, Edinburgh]

LAC   Libraries & Archives, Canada

M   Mull, the Island and its People, [Edinburgh, 2001]

MB   The MacLeans of Boreray

MH   Montreal Herald, series

NARA   National Archives, Records Administration

NCSA   North Carolina State Archives

NLS   National Library of Scotland

NSARM   Nova Scotia, Archives Records Management

NRS   National Records of Scotland, [Edinburgh]

PAC   Public Archives, Canada

PANS   Public Archives, Nova Scotia

PAPEI   Public Archives, Prince Edward Island

SCA   Scottish Catholic Archives

SG   Scottish Genealogist, series

PEOPLE OF THE HEBRIDES, 1800-1850

SM Scots Magazine, series

SP Skye Pioneers and the Island

TML The MacLeods

TNA The National Archives

W Witness, series

Emigrant ships from the Hebrides, 1790-1850

Ann	Stornoway	1828	Cape Breton
Commerce	Tobermory	1822	Nova Scotia
Economy	Tobermory	1819	Nova Scotia
Emperor Alexr.	Tobermory	1823	Cape Breton
Harmony	Barra	1821	Cape Breton
Humphreys	Tobermory	1806	Prince Edward Island
Isle of Skye	Tobermory	1806	Prince Edward Island
Malay	Skye	1830	Nova Scotia
Monarch	Tobermory	1823	Quebec
Oughton	Uist	1803	Prince Edward Island
Oughton	Uist	1804	Quebec
Polly	Skye	1803	Prince Edward Island
Prince of Wales	Stornaway	1813	Hudson Bay
Universe	Stornaway	1828	Cape Breton
William Tell	Barra	1817	Nova Scotia